THE GREAT AMERICAN Birthday Cake BOOK

THE GREAT AMERICAN Birthday Cake Book

CAKE DESIGNER Jazmine Nixon

RECIPES Dean Brettschneider

EDITOR Wendy Nixon

weldon**owen**

Jazmine NIXON

CAKE DESIGNER

&

DEAN BRETTSCHNEIDER

BAKER

$\mathcal{I}$ took my first tentative steps into the world of cake decorating five years ago, when a friend asked me to bake and decorate her cake for her twenty-first birthday. To this day, I am not sure why either of us thought this was a good idea, as I had never made anything more advanced than chocolate cupcakes and certainly not a two-tiered cake covered in fondant.

To my relief, the cake was a great success, and it wasn't long before I was being asked to make special-occasion cakes every week. I quickly fell in love with the process of creating something delicious and unique for each person.

It was a blessing creating the cakes for this book alongside my lovely mother-in-law, Wendy, in her gorgeous kitchen (well, it was gorgeous until this project started and her house became Birthday Cake Central!). Over eight weeks we baked more than 100 cakes; measured out pounds of powdered sugar, candies, fondant, chocolate, and licorice; worked on cakes in various stages of completion on Wendy's kitchen counter and down the hallway; and then photographed them in her living room. It was a joy to spend so many messy hours together, side by side.

Even though decorating cakes is my passion and I could think about it all day long, this project had to fit around my full-time "real" job as a graphic designer. It was full on; we burned the midnight oil on weeknights and weekends. We shared many laughs and frustrations, but most of all we had a lot of fun.

Every week the courier would eagerly pop his head in the door to see our latest creation, but it was the visiting children who always made our day. Thinking they had stepped into a fairy tale, they would look longingly at the finished cakes and immediately start planning their next birthday party. After a little visitor proclaimed the pink castle to be a "magical kingdom," we were inspired to ask a class of six- and seven-year-olds to name all the cakes. As you can see, they have great imaginations!

Planning, baking, and decorating a cake is a wonderful way to celebrate a special occasion, and I hope you will take these recipes and make them your own. It brings me great joy to think of all the wonderful memories that you will make as you create something just right for your loved ones.

Have fun, and eat cake!

Jaz

BEFORE YOU BEGIN

You've chosen a cake and you're ready to start baking it. Before you begin, however, it's important to read through the individual instructions, making sure you have all the necessary equipment and ingredients. Take your time, follow the directions step-by-step, and be aware that some decorations need to be made a day or two in advance of decorating the cake. Finally, and most importantly, only start frosting and decorating a cake once it has cooled completely—it would be a shame to see all your hard work slide off the cake!

Baking the Cake

If you are short on time, feel free to purchase a premade cake, but make sure it is the same size as the one recommended in the instructions.

I do, however, recommend that you bake your own cake, as the two recipes supplied here by professional baker and pâtissier Dean Brettschneider (globalbaker.com) are not only delicious but also ideal for carving or stacking into the cake of your choice.

Before you start baking, there are a few things to consider.

- If possible, use an electric mixer (rather than a food processor) or an electric hand mixer.
- Successful baking is all about accuracy, so electronic scales are best.

SELECTING BAKING PANS

The following baking pans have been used in this book:

- Round: 6-, 8-, 10-inch.
- Rectangle: 9-by-13-inch.
- Hemisphere: I used a pan with an 8-inch base and a depth of 4 inches.
- Princess cake: I used a traditional Wilton wonder mold pan with a base diameter of 8 inches and a height of 5 inches, but a traditional princess cake mold will also work.
- I lined muffin pans with paper liners to make cupcakes.

(Hemisphere, Wilton wonder mold, and princess cake pans can be found at cake decorating stores and online.)

PREPARING YOUR PANS

There are two ways to prepare your pans to avoid your cake sticking:

1. Grease liberally with cooking spray.
2. Grease liberally with cooking spray, then line with parchment paper and spray again.

Notes

The removable base of a springform cake pan can be lined with either aluminum foil or parchment paper before spraying with cooking spray.

For cupcakes, it is easier to pour the mixture into the cupcake liners inside the muffin pan, using a pitcher, than it is to try to spoon it in.

MIXING YOUR INGREDIENTS

Follow these simple rules to ensure baking success:

- Accuracy is key, so level off spoon or cup measurements and use scale measurements for weight.
- Sifting dry ingredients helps to aerate a mixture, keeping it light and helping the cake to rise.
- Wait for melted butter to cool before adding it to a mixture so as to avoid cooking the eggs when all the ingredients are mixed together.

COOKING YOUR CAKE

The cooking times in this book vary according to each cake's size and shape. Refer to each cake's individual instructions for specific cooking times.

- Recipe cooking times are only a guide and vary depending on your oven. It's a good idea to take notes on the cooking time to refer to if you bake the cake again.
- Regular bake is preferable to convection bake, because convection bake can cause the cake to peak in the center. If you do use convection bake, reduce the temperature given in the recipe by 70°F.
- Once the cake is in the oven, resist the urge to open the door until at least three-quarters of the way through the cooking time, otherwise your cake may collapse or

sink. Tilt the door slightly open toward the end of the cooking time to quickly check your cake's progress, before closing the door again.

- Set the timer for three-quarters of the way through the cooking time. Then, for the last quarter of the cooking time, adjust the timer in 5–10 minute increments until your cake is cooked through.

- If you know your cake isn't cooked through but it's golden and crusty on top, carefully place a sheet of aluminum foil on top of the cake to prevent it from over-browning while still allowing the cake to continue cooking until it's fully done.

- To test that your cake is cooked through, press your finger gently into the center of the cake. If it is cooked, it will bounce back. Alternatively, insert a skewer into the center of the cake. If it comes out clean, your cake is cooked through.

COOLING THE CAKE

Never decorate a cake until it is completely cool. Follow these simple steps:

- Leave the cake to cool in the pan for 10–30 minutes before turning it out onto a cooling rack.

- Before turning a cake out onto a cooling rack, run a sharp knife around the inside edges first to help loosen it. If it struggles to come loose, tap the top of the pan with a knife when it is upside down.

Storing the Cake

Unfrosted cakes will keep in an airtight container for 2–3 days. Cupcakes will keep for 1–2 days.

Once frosted, keep your cake in a cool, dry place out of direct sunlight. The frosting seals in the freshness.

FREEZING & DEFROSTING

It is common practice to freeze cakes before decorating them. (They cannot be frozen after frosting or decorating.) This keeps the cake fresh and reduces the workload of making the cake and decorating it all in one day.

- As a rule, allow one day for cooking the cake and another day for defrosting and decorating.

- Even if you are not planning to freeze the cake, it is a good idea to bake it the day before decorating it, as it will be easier to work with. Once cool, wrap with plastic wrap or store in an airtight container. To prepare the cake for freezing, wrap the completely cooled cake first in aluminum foil and then in plastic wrap. This will prevent the cake from drying out.

- To defrost your cake, thaw it overnight (still wrapped) in the refrigerator, or leave it on a counter at room temperature until defrosted. Depending on the size of the cake, this should take about 3 hours.

Carving & Shaping the Cake

Resist the urge to start carving or shaping your cake until it is completely cool, otherwise you might find that a chunk or two comes off at the same time!

- When shaping or slicing a cake, it's best to use a sharp serrated knife. Wipe the blade with a damp cloth between each slice to keep the slices clean.

- It is always better to carve a little at a time than to carve too much!

Serving the Cake

Before serving the cake, make sure that you have removed any toothpicks, skewers, floral wire, and flower picks that were being used to assemble the cake.

RECIPES

Both cake recipes provided—vanilla and chocolate—are easy to bake in standard round and rectangle pans. You can choose your preferred flavor for each birthday cake recipe, except where indicated (for example, chocolate cake crumbs are needed for The Dirty Digger's dirt, see page 116). However, for hemisphere pans, I recommend using the chocolate cake recipe, as the vanilla cake's longer cooking time makes it difficult to release from the pan. For best results, I recommend that you measure (or weigh) the ingredients carefully.

Vanilla Cake & Cupcakes

PREP TIME: 30 MINUTES

	6-inch round or 12 cupcakes	8-inch round	10-inch round or 9-by-13-inch rectangle
INGREDIENTS			
butter	⅔ cup (5 oz)	1¼ cups (10 oz)	1¾ cups (14 oz)
white chocolate chips	½ cup (3 oz)	1 cup (6 oz)	1¼ cups (8 oz)
superfine sugar	1 cup (8 oz)	2 cups (16 oz)	3 cups (22 oz)
whole milk	⅔ cup (5½ fl oz)	1⅓ cups (11 fl oz)	2 cups (15 fl oz)
vanilla extract	¾ tsp	1½ tsp	2 tsp
all-purpose flour	1 cup (¼ lb)	1⅓ cups (½ lb)	2 cups (10½ oz)
self-rising flour	¾ cup (3½ oz)	1½ cups (7 oz)	2 cups (10 oz)
eggs, lightly beaten	2 large	4 large	5 large
BAKE TIME	6-inch round: 1 hour 25 min	8-inch round: 1 hour 40 min	10-inch round: 1 hour 50 min
	cupcakes: 20 min		rectangle: 1 hour 15 min

This cake has a white-chocolate base and can be carved and cut easily.

Bake the cake at least a day before you plan to decorate it.

Preheat the oven to 325°F on standard bake (275°–285°F on convection bake, but avoid using convection bake as it causes excessive peaking during baking). Prepare cake pan (see page 10).

Combine butter, white chocolate chips, superfine sugar, milk, and vanilla extract in a large heatproof bowl set over a pot of simmering water until everything has melted together and the sugar is dissolved. Remove from the heat and set aside for 10 minutes to cool down slightly.

In a separate bowl, sift the two flours together, then stir into the melted mixture along with the lightly beaten eggs. Mix gently until the mixture is smooth and free of lumps.

Pour the mixture into the prepared pan (see page 10), filling it no more than two-thirds full so there is enough room for the cake to bake as it rises. Bake according to the times listed above, checking the cake regularly during the last quarter of cooking time, or until a skewer comes out clean when inserted into the cake.

Cool the cake in the pan for 30 minutes, then turn it out onto a wire rack to cool. Once fully cooled, wrap the cake in plastic wrap or place it in an airtight container if you plan to decorate it the following day, or wrap it in aluminum foil followed by plastic wrap and then freeze it.

Note

If you know your cake isn't cooked through but it's golden and crusty on top, carefully place a sheet of aluminum foil on top of the cake. This will stop it from getting any darker on top but will allow it to continue cooking until it's fully done.

Chocolate Cake & Cupcakes

PREP TIME: 30 MINUTES

	6-inch round or 12 cupcakes	8-inch round or 8-inch hemisphere	10-inch round or 9-by-13-inch rectangle or princess cake
INGREDIENTS			
milk	½ cup (4 fl oz)	¾ cup (8 fl oz)	1¼ cups (10½ fl oz)
cream of tartar	½ tsp	¾ tsp	1¼ tsp
oil	¼ cup (2 fl oz)	⅓ cup (4 fl oz)	½ cup (5½ fl oz)
eggs, lightly beaten	1 large	2 large	3 large
vanilla extract	¾ tsp	1¼ tsp	2 tsp
all-purpose flour	1 cup (5 oz)	1½ cups (9½ oz)	2¼ cups (13 oz)
unsweetened cocoa powder	½ cup (1¾ oz)	¾ cup (3½ oz)	1¼ cups (5 oz)
superfine sugar	1 cup (7½ oz)	1½ cups (15½ oz)	2¼ cups (20 oz)
baking soda	¾ tsp	1¼ tsp	2 tsp
baking powder	½ tsp	¾ tsp	1 tsp
hot water	¼ cup (2½ fl oz)	⅓ cup (5 fl oz)	½ cup (7 fl oz)
BAKE TIME	6-inch round: 45 min	8-inch round: 1 hour 15 min	10-inch round: 1 hour 15 min
	cupcakes: 20 min	hemisphere: 1 hour 15 min	rectangle: 1 hour 10 min
			princess cake: 1 hour 20 min

Bake the cake at least a day before you plan to decorate it.

Preheat the oven to 350°F on standard bake (325°F on convection bake, but avoid using convection bake as it causes excessive peaking during baking). Prepare cake pan (see page 10).

Place milk and cream of tartar in a small glass, stir, and set aside for 5 minutes. In a small bowl, place oil, eggs, and vanilla extract and stir to combine.

In a large mixing bowl, sift flour, cocoa powder, superfine sugar, baking soda, and baking powder.

Scrape all of the milk mixture into the egg mixture and stir, then add the wet ingredients to the dry ingredients. Using a hand mixer, mix to combine, then slowly add hot water and mix well until you have a smooth batter.

Pour the mixture into the prepared pan (see page 10), filling it no more than two-thirds full so there is enough room for the cake to bake as it rises. Bake according to the times listed above, checking the cake regularly during the last quarter of cooking time, or until a skewer comes out clean when inserted into the cake.

Cool for 15 minutes in the pan, then remove and cool completely on a wire rack. Once fully cool, wrap the cake in plastic wrap or place it in an airtight container if you plan to decorate it the following day, or wrap it in aluminum foil, followed by plastic wrap, and then freeze it.

Note

If you know your cake isn't cooked through but it's crusty on top, carefully place a sheet of aluminum foil on top of the cake. This will stop it from getting any darker on top but will allow it to continue cooking until it's fully done.

Gingerbread

PREP TIME: 15 MINUTES PLUS CUTTING OUT SHAPES

INGREDIENTS

5 oz (1¼ sticks) butter

⅔ cup (13 oz) golden syrup or corn syrup

5 cups (25 oz) all-purpose flour

1¼ cups (8½ oz) superfine sugar

2 tbsp (½ oz) ground ginger

1 tbsp (¼ oz) baking soda

1 large egg

Melt butter and golden syrup or corn syrup together in a microwave-proof bowl in the microwave or in a small saucepan over a very low heat.

Sift flour, superfine sugar, ground ginger, and baking soda together in a large mixing bowl.

Whisk eggs in a small bowl and add to the dry ingredients along with the melted butter and golden syrup. Mix to combine, then leave the mixture to cool until it reaches room temperature.

Wrap dough in plastic wrap and leave for 1 hour. Preheat oven to 350°F.

Remove dough from plastic wrap. Lightly dust your work surface with flour and roll the dough out until it's approximately ⅜ inch thick. Cut into desired shapes. Lay out all of the gingerbread pieces on a lined baking sheet and place in the fridge or freezer for 10–15 minutes (this helps the pieces to hold their shape while cooking).

Remove from fridge, place in the preheated oven, and bake until golden brown (cooking time depends on the sizes and shapes). Set your timer and watch carefully from approximately 10 minutes onward.

Note

Gingerbread dough can be made in advance. Wrap the dough in plastic wrap until it's airtight, then refrigerate it for up to a week.

Rice Krispies Treats

The Rice Krispies Treats mixture provides an alternative to cake. Not only is the mixture quick and easy to make, but it's also both strong and light and can be carved easily or molded into shapes.

INGREDIENTS

mini marshmallows

Rice Krispies

(refer to the individual instructions for each cake for quantities)

If you are going to press the Rice Krispies Treats into molds or bowls, prepare them before you start by spraying liberally with cooking spray.

In a large saucepan over a low-to-medium heat, melt the marshmallows, stirring continuously. Initially, it will appear as if nothing is happening, then all of a sudden the marshmallows will melt. Quickly remove the saucepan from the heat and stir in Rice Krispies.

When the mixture is cool enough to handle, act fast, as you'll only have a few minutes to work with the mixture before it cools and hardens. The mixture is incredibly sticky, so spray your hands with cooking spray first, then press the mixture tightly into prepared molds, or mold the mixture into your desired shape and set it aside on parchment paper to cool and set.

Don't worry if your molded shapes are not perfect; once the Rice Krispies Treats have hardened, you can carve and shave a more precise shape with a serrated knife. The Rice Krispies give the surface a bumpy texture but that will be hidden once covered in buttercream or ganache.

Meringue Kisses

PREP TIME: 40 MINUTES. YIELD: 140 (APPROX.) KISSES

INGREDIENTS

4 egg whites

2 cups (12 oz) superfine sugar

colors and flavors as indicated on
individual cake-decorating pages

Make the meringue kisses at least a day before you plan to decorate the cake. Meringues will keep well for up to a week if stored in an airtight container.

Preheat oven to 250°F.

Put the egg whites and superfine sugar into a glass or metal bowl set over a pan of gently simmering water (don't boil the water as this will cook the egg whites). Stir until the sugar is dissolved and the mixture is warm to the touch.

Transfer the mixture to the bowl of an electric mixer. Then, using the whisk attachment, whisk until thick and cool. This should take approximately 15 minutes, and the meringue should hold stiff peaks.

To make the multicolored striped kisses on the #6 cake (see page 196), follow the recipe's coloring instructions before piping.

To make the kisses for the Meringue Frenzy, read the instructions on page 185, then continue with this recipe.

Line 3 baking sheets with parchment paper. Use small blobs of the meringue mixture to stick down the parchment paper in the corners of each sheet.

To ensure the kisses are all the same size, draw 1¼-inch circles (about the size of a quarter) onto parchment paper and use these as a guide when you pipe each kiss. Fill the piping bag with the meringue mixture (for the Meringue Frenzy on page 185, fill the bag only one-third full at a time, adding flavorings and toppings as indicated) and pipe small kisses, keeping them as uniform as possible. To make a kiss shape, squeeze until the circle is the size of the base you want, then release the pressure and pull up to create a peak on the kiss.

Place the trays of kisses into the preheated oven and bake for 1 hour with the door slightly ajar to allow moisture to escape. Then turn the oven off, and keeping the door ajar, leave the kisses to dry out in the oven overnight.

The following day, remove the kisses from the baking sheet and either store in an airtight container until use (up to a week) or use them to decorate your cake.

Sugar Syrup

Sugar syrup is used as the "glue" when making sugared flowers and fruit.

INGREDIENTS

1 cup superfine sugar

1 cup water

Combine sugar and water in a small saucepan and bring to a simmer over medium heat, stirring constantly until the sugar is dissolved. Simmer the syrup for 3–5 minutes or until the sugar is dissolved. Remove from the heat and leave to cool.

Brush the syrup on flowers and fruit using a pastry brush before sprinkling or rolling them in sugar. This gives the fruit and flowers a frosted appearance.

Candy Decorations

If you are unable to find the candy called for to decorate a cake, feel free to substitute another type of candy. One of the joys of cake decorating is that it's a creative endeavor, so have fun with it!

1

2

3

4

9

8

12

18

14

15

19

13

21

22

23

30

28

29

31

EQUIPMENT

1. Hemisphere pan
2. Offset palette knife/spatula
3. Cake board
4. Turntable
5. Icing smoother
6. Cupcake liners
7. Cake leveler
8. Paddle attachment
9. Whisk attachment
10. Mini shape cutters
11. Palette knife/spatula
12. Rolling pin
13. Pastry brush
14. Daisy-shape cutter
15. Hydrangea cutters
16. Alphabet cutters
17. Pins
18. Sponge
19. Toothpicks
20. Paintbrushes
21. Piping tip
22. Small coupler
23. Flower picks
24. Straw
25. Skewer
26. Dowels
27. Wire cutters
28. Wonder mold (princess cake pan)
29. Can cutter*
30. Fondant smoother
31. Piping bag
32. Floral wire
33. Small silicone mat

*Make by cutting the lid off a standard 14-oz can

CAKE PREPARATION

Leveling

Leveling a cake is the process of slicing the natural dome off the top so it is flat and easy to stack and frost. It also gives the top of your cake a smooth, sharp edge. For best results, always let the cake cool before leveling it.

Once leveled, turn the cake over (base side up) before frosting, as the base naturally has a more level surface. Also, since the base has not been cut, fewer crumbs will get into your frosting.

There are two ways to level a cake. I recommend using a cake leveler if possible (see Equipment, page 17).

USING A CAKE LEVELER

These are available from specialty cake-decorating stores and online. As well as being more accurate, using a cake leveler means you can ensure that each cake in a stack is exactly the same height.

Place the cake on a flat surface, dome side up. Stand the cake leveler beside the cake and adjust the cutting wire so it is the same height as the base of the dome (where the side of the cake and dome meet). Adjust the cutting wire by moving the ends of the wire up or down the cake-leveler frame. Keeping the frame of the cake leveler upright and on the flat surface on either side of the cake, use a gentle sawing motion to pull the wire through the cake. If the crust is hard, you might need to make a small cut at the beginning, using a sharp serrated knife, to help the wire to enter the cake.

USING A KNIFE

Place the cake on a flat surface or turntable, dome side up. Using a sharp serrated knife, gently saw off the dome, keeping the knife as level as possible as you cut. This method does not require any specialty equipment, but it can be difficult to achieve an even, flat surface. You may like to wrap a thick ribbon or length of parchment paper around the cake (secured with a toothpick or pin) to use as a level guide when cutting.

Cupcakes are easy to level with a serrated knife, as the cupcake wrapper is an easy guide for cutting evenly.

Stacking & Filling

Make sure leveled cakes have been turned over (base side up). Take the first cake for the stack and evenly spread frosting over the top surface, then place the next layer on top. Repeat with all layers. It is up to you how much frosting you use between your cake layers. Generally I spread enough frosting on each layer so that a little spills out the side when the next layer is stacked on top (not too much though, or your cake layers could slide right off).

Crumb Coating

A crumb coat is simply a thin base layer of frosting on your cake to seal in the crumbs, preventing them from showing through your final coat of frosting. While this step is not essential, it will make a big difference to the look of your final product. You do not need to crumb coat your cake if you are covering the cake with candies or fondant, as you will not see the crumbs anyway.

For the crumb coat, use the same frosting that will be used for the final coat. Apply it with a palette knife or offset spatula to achieve a very thin, smooth finish (you should be able to see the cake through the frosting). Never wipe excess crumb-coat frosting back into the main bowl as it will be full of crumbs and will spoil the rest of the frosting. Ensure the crumb coat is dry to the touch before applying the final layer of frosting. This will take 20–30 minutes in the fridge or longer at room temperature.

Creating a Smooth Finish

Once the crumb coat is dry to the touch, use a palette knife or offset spatula to apply frosting thickly all over the cake. To smooth out the sides, hold your spatula or icing scraper straight up and down against the side of the cake. Using even pressure, drag the spatula or icing scraper around the side of the cake, occasionally wiping excess frosting off with a damp cloth, so there isn't too much build up. Once you have scraped all the way around the cake, fill in any holes or uneven spots with the leftover frosting. Repeat the smoothing process again until you are happy that the surface is evenly coated.

When covering a round cake to a smooth finish, it is helpful to use a turntable. This allows you to hold your spatula or icing scraper flat against the cake while slowly turning the turntable. Once the sides are smooth, use an offset spatula to pull the excess frosting around the top edge of the cake into the center. This is the best way to create a clean, sharp edge on the cake.

Supporting a Stack

When a smaller stack of cakes is layered on a wider stack of cakes, the weight of the top tier needs to be supported.

Insert a skewer or dowel all the way down into the largest bottom cake and use a pen or a knife to mark the skewer where it enters the cake. Pull out the skewer and cut the skewer where marked. Using your first skewer as a guide, cut four more skewers to the same length and push them into the cake: one in the middle then four surrounding the central skewer halfway between the center and the outside edge of the cake. The top of the skewers should be flush with the top of the cake.

Stick the smaller cake stack to a cake board the same size as the cake with buttercream or ganache and place on top of the larger cake stack. The weight of the smaller cake will be supported by the skewers in the larger cake underneath.

Stencils

All the stencils you need to make these cakes are provided in the lift-out sheets in the pocket at the back of this book. Always trace the stencil you need onto parchment paper so you can keep the original stencil for next time.

Sometimes the designs are large and require pieces to be cut from multiple cakes, then jigsawed together. The dashed lines on the stencils represent where separate pieces of cake need to be stuck together with frosting to form a bigger shape.

Melting Chocolate

Chocolate can be melted on the stovetop or in a microwave.

- To melt chocolate on the stovetop, bring a small amount of water to a simmer in a small saucepan. Place the chocolate in a glass or stainless steel bowl set over the saucepan. Stir the chocolate constantly with a wooden spoon until melted, taking care not to get any water in the chocolate.

- To melt chocolate in a microwave, place chocolate in a microwave-proof bowl. Heat in 30-second bursts, stirring in between, until melted.

Coloring Coconut

Colored coconut is marvelous to use for creating texture, such as for grass and feathers. Place shredded coconut into a large zippered plastic bag and add a few drops of liquid food coloring. Seal, shake, and massage the bag gently with your hands until the color is evenly distributed. Add more color if necessary and repeat until your desired color is reached.

Cutting Sugar Wafers

When cutting sugar wafers into shapes, use the tip of a knife to make tiny cuts rather than sawing across the wafer, which will make it break. (I learned this the hard way!)

Ice Cream Cones

Ice cream cones come in three shapes:

- Sugar cone: This cone generally has a waffle pattern and no shape in the cup at the top.

- Standard ice cream cone: This is a pointed cone with a bowl-shaped cup at the top.

- Flat-based standard ice cream cone: This cone is a standard ice cream cone with a flat base that the cone can stand upon.

Separating Giant Licorice Allsorts

Giant licorice allsorts can be gently separated into layers of small black licorice and colored squares. If necessary, they can be gently washed in warm water, wiped with a paper towel, and left to air-dry.

FROSTING

I have used four types of frosting in this book: buttercream (also known as Vienna cream), royal icing, ganache, and fondant. Each has a different consistency and flavor and produces a different result. It is always advisable to keep a little buttercream, ganache, or royal icing aside for final touch-ups and attachments.

Buttercream

Buttercream is a creamy and fluffy frosting that is perfect for both piping and spreading.

INGREDIENTS

9 oz (2½ sticks) butter, at room temperature,
   or 1¼ cups (9 oz) vegetable shortening
6 cups (1½ lb) powdered sugar
2 tbsp milk

Beat butter or vegetable shortening with an electric mixer, using the paddle attachment, until the butter lightens in color or the vegetable shortening softens. Slowly add powdered sugar in small batches (so it doesn't fly out of the mixing bowl), beating in between until combined. Add milk 1 tablespoon at a time. If using vegetable shortening, you may require more than 2 tablespoons of milk.

Notes

The key to success is to start with room-temperature butter (not melted) and to beat with an electric mixer until the butter turns from a yellow to a white tone before adding powdered sugar.

Before using buttercream, especially for piping, beat it again if necessary so it is as light, fluffy, and soft as possible.

Vegetable shortening is a colorless vegetable fat that can be used instead of butter for a dairy-free option. It also allows you to create pure colors that would otherwise get tainted by the color of the butter. For example, if making purple buttercream, the yellow of the butter turns the icing a brown-gray color rather than bright purple, and light blue colors take on a green tone.

Although a different flavor than butter, vegetable shortening is still delicious.

Buttercream can be stored in an airtight container for up to 2 weeks in the fridge, but bring it back to room temperature and beat again before using.

Buttercream is affected by the weather, so occasionally you may need to add a little more milk to make it softer, or more powdered sugar to make it stiffer. The amount of food coloring will affect the consistency of the mix. If a dark or bright color is required, gel coloring is a better option, as the color is more intense and a little goes a long way (for Coloring, see page 24). Flavors can also be added to buttercream using extracts, oils, syrups, and powders. Just be careful how much extra liquid you are adding, and use less milk if necessary.

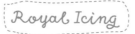

Royal Icing

Royal icing is made with egg whites or meringue powder and dries hard, so it is wonderful for piping.

INGREDIENTS

1 egg white or 1 tbsp meringue powder mixed with 5 tsp
   warm water
2 cups (8½ oz) powdered sugar, sifted
1 tsp lemon juice

Beat egg white with an electric mixer, using the whisk attachment, on a slow speed until bubbles start to appear. Add sifted powdered sugar a little at a time, beating on a higher speed until it forms firm peaks. Add lemon juice and mix in gently. Tightly cover the icing with plastic wrap as soon as it is made so it doesn't dry out.

There are two consistencies of royal icing: piping consistency and flood consistency.

- Piping consistency (the standard recipe) is spreadable but able to hold a peak.

- Flood consistency is runnier and will spread out to dry in a smooth "pool." Add a couple of drops of water to the standard royal icing mixture and stir. To test that it has reached flood consistency, scoop up a spoonful of icing, then drizzle it over the bowl of icing. If all the drop lines spread out and become smooth again within 15 seconds, then the icing is at flood consistency. If not, repeat the process again, adding a couple of drops of water each time and repeating the 15-second test after each addition.

Notes

A spray bottle can be used to add water very slowly. An overly wet mixture cannot be rectified by adding more powdered sugar. Only the addition of piping-consistency royal icing will stiffen it up again.

Humidity will slow the drying process. Royal icing takes 8–12 hours to fully set all the way through, although it will be dry to the touch before that. The thinner you apply it, the sooner it will dry! Once set, royal icing decorations will keep indefinitely.

Leftover royal icing will keep in an airtight container in the fridge for up to 10 days. Remove from the fridge, bring to room temperature, and stir well before using.

Ganache

Ganache is made by melting dark, milk, or white chocolate and cream together. It is a good idea to make it a day or two in advance (unless instructions specify not to) to allow for cooling time and to save time on decorating day! Covered in the fridge, it will keep for up to 2 weeks.

INGREDIENTS

2¼ cups (14 oz) chocolate chips or disks (milk, dark, or white)
¾ cup (6¾ fl oz) heavy cream

Place a medium-size stainless steel bowl over a saucepan of simmering water. Add the chocolate and cream to the bowl and stir continuously with a wooden spoon until the chocolate has just melted and is combined with the cream to a nice glossy finish. Remove the bowl from the heat.

Notes

For dark ganache, I recommend using chocolate that is 60–70 percent cocoa.

If using ganache from the fridge, allow time to bring it back to room temperature, then mix well. It should be the consistency of toothpaste—not runny, not solid, and just a little sticky. If it is too hard to stir, warm it slightly by giving it short 10-second bursts in the microwave or, alternatively, in a heatproof bowl over a saucepan of simmering water. If it is too runny, leave it to cool in the fridge.

Fondant

Fondant icing is similar in texture to modeling clay and needs to be kneaded and softened with your hands before rolling. You can buy fondant in a range of colors from supermarkets, cake-decorating stores, and online. Be aware that different brands have slightly different consistencies and flavors.

Here are a few things to remember:

- Always knead your fondant until soft and pliable before rolling or modeling.

- Knead on a clean surface dusted with cornstarch (to prevent fondant from sticking).

- Work quickly to avoid the fondant drying out and cracking. Any leftover fondant needs to be covered in plastic wrap or sealed in a zippered plastic bag.

- Never put a fondant-covered cake in the fridge, as it will sweat. Instead, keep it in a cool, dry place out of direct sunlight. The fondant seals in the cake's freshness.

ROLLING OUT FONDANT

Fondant must be kneaded to become soft and pliable before being rolled out. Always dust the surface you are working on and any tool (such as a rolling pin) with cornstarch to prevent the fondant from sticking. Make sure the surface is clean and free of crumbs, and stop every so often to re-dust it if necessary.

- "Thinly roll out" fondant means to roll it out to a thickness of ⅛ inch.

- "Roll out" fondant means to roll it out to a thickness of ¼ inch.

Notes

It is preferable when rolling out fondant to use a fondant rolling pin, as its smooth silicone surface gives a professional finish.

It is a good idea to roll fondant out on a large silicone or vinyl mat, as this not only prevents the fondant from sticking to the counter, but it also makes it easier to transport the fondant to the cake for covering. If your fondant is hot or sticky, you may also want to dust the mat with a little cornstarch before starting.

COVERING A CAKE WITH FONDANT

1. Once you have rolled the fondant out on the silicone or vinyl mat, place the mat and fondant upside down over the center of the frosted cake so that the mat is facing up. Carefully peel the mat back from the fondant. Alternatively, if you are not using a mat, roll the sheet of fondant over a cornstarch-dusted rolling pin, then slowly unroll it over the cake. The fondant should look like a tablecloth draped over a table. Once the fondant is on the cake, secure the top edges first by gently pressing the fondant layer onto the frosted cake using your fingertips.

2. To smooth the sides, start at the top and work your way around the cake, lifting the draped icing with one hand and smoothing 1–1½ inches of the fondant up and in with the other hand. Continue this motion down the cake until all the folds disappear. (Smoothing the fondant up and in seems illogical but this is the best way to remove any draping.)

3. Using a sharp knife, trim off the excess fondant around the bottom edge (as shown below) and then polish the fondant to a smooth finish with a fondant smoother (dusted with cornstarch if necessary).

4. Prick any air bubbles under the fondant with a pin and press out the air with a fondant smoother. Hold one fondant smoother on the top and one on the side of the cake. Applying gentle pressure, slide them toward each other until they meet at the edge of the cake. This will create a sharp edge. Trim any excess fondant from the bottom edge.

Don't worry: It seems difficult the first time, but practice makes perfect!

FONDANT BOW

1. Roll out fondant to ⅛–¼ inch thick. Cut out 2 rectangles 3 by 5½ inches and 1 rectangle 1¼ by 3 inches.

2. Pinch the ends of each rectangle together.

3. Roll 2 paper towels into cylinder shapes about ¾ inch in diameter. Fold each long rectangle over a paper towel. Squeeze the pinched ends together.

4. Drape the small rectangle over the pinched ends of the bow loops. Stand upright to dry.

COLORING

I would love to be standing beside you in your kitchen as you color your frosting, telling you to add quite a lot of this one, a little of that, and a tiny amount of the next. It is very difficult to give specific instructions regarding the amount used to make a color as it varies according to the volume of frosting you are making.

The size of the circles will give you an idea of proportions, but remember this is just a guide. Start with a very small amount of color, mix it well into your frosting and see whether or not you are close to achieving the color you desire. Then keep adding the colors, a little at a time, proportionate to the size shown in the circles. As you will see, some colors, such as yellow, need a lot of food coloring added while others, like pale pink, need as much as will fit on the tip of a toothpick. Good luck, go slowly, and remember, you can always add more!

There are two types of food coloring: liquid and gel. Liquid food coloring is great for making pale colors and is readily available from your supermarket. However, if too much is added, it can make your frosting runny or sticky. Liquid food coloring is generally used with buttercream frosting.

Gel food coloring has a more concentrated color and a thicker consistency. It is preferable for using in royal icing and fondant, but it can also be used to color buttercream.

When using liquid or gel food coloring, always add a small amount of coloring at a time, such as a drop from a toothpick dipped into the bottle. Mix your coloring in well, then add more if necessary. It's amazing how far a little color goes. Once it is added, it can't be removed!

Dark and bright colors require a lot of food coloring. Black, red, and brown are the hardest colors to create. When making black or dark brown, it is best to start with a brown base by adding cocoa powder to the frosting before coloring. This will reduce the amount of food coloring required. Colors can intensify over time, so if possible give them a chance to darken.

A variety of colors can be achieved by mixing a few base colors together. However, you can also purchase the color you want from cake-decorating stores or online.

Note

Keep gel coloring pots fresh by using a toothpick or ice pick to scoop out the gel. This way, you won't contaminate and ruin the contents.

Maroon
- Red
- Black

Red
- Red

Terra-cotta
- Cocoa*
- Red
- Yellow
- Black

Light green
- Yellow
- Blue
or
- Green

Green
- Yellow
- Blue
or
- Green

Dark green
- Yellow
- Blue
or
- Green

Turquoise
- Yellow
- Blue

Dusty blue
- Blue
- Black

Pale ice blue
- Blue

Navy blue
- Blue
- Black

Indigo/Dark purple
- Blue
- Red

Purple
- Blue
- Red

Peach
- Red
- Yellow

Sand
- Red
- Yellow
- Black

Light brown
- Cocoa*
- Red
- Yellow
- Black

Orange

- Red
- Yellow

Yellow

- Yellow

Lemon

- Yellow

Khaki

- Cocoa*
- Yellow
- Blue
- Black

Dusty green

- Yellow
- Blue
- Black

Mint green

- Yellow
- Blue

Light blue

- Blue

Medium blue

- Blue

Blue

- Blue

Violet/Light purple

- Blue
- Red

Pink

- Red

Pale pink

- Red

Black

- Cocoa*
- Black

Dark gray

- Black

Gray

- Black

COLORING FONDANT

There are two different ways to color fondant:

- Begin with white fondant. Add small amounts of gel coloring and knead the fondant to mix the color through evenly. Be careful not to add too much, as excess liquid will make the fondant sticky.

- Buy precolored fondant and mix different colors together. Precolored fondants have very concentrated colors. This option can save you a lot of time compared to gel coloring and kneading. You can mix precolored fondants together or with white fondant to achieve a range of colors.

* For all frosting types requiring cocoa powder, add the cocoa first to create a brown base before adding other coloring.

PIPING TIPS & COUPLERS

1. Large coupler base
2. Large coupler ring
3. Small coupler base
4. Small coupler ring
5. Extra-large round Wilton 1A
6. Medium petal Wilton 104
7. Leaf tip Wilton 352
8. Extra-small round Wilton 2
9. Small star Wilton 30
10. Extra-large star Wilton 1M
11. Large round Wilton 6
12. Medium round Wilton 4
13. Small round Wilton 3
14. Small petal Wilton 102
15. Basket-weave Wilton 47
16. Large open star Wilton 199
17. Grass/multi-opening Wilton 233

PIPING

Piping is a traditional cake-decorating technique that requires patience, practice, and a steady hand. Squeezing frosting out through differently shaped tips allows you to create an assortment of patterns and effects.

Piping Tips & Couplers

Piping tips are small metal cones with different-shaped holes in the narrow end that produce shapes when frosting or royal icing is pushed through them (see equipment pictured opposite). They can be found at supermarkets, cake-decorating stores, and online.

I use Wilton brand tips, but there are many other brands with equivalent tips. The following tips are just a guide; have fun experimenting with whatever tips you can.

ROUND TIPS

Extra-small – Wilton 2
Small – Wilton 3
Medium – Wilton 4
Large – Wilton 6
Extra-large – Wilton 1A

PETAL TIPS

Small – Wilton 102
Medium – Wilton 104

STAR TIPS

Small – Wilton 30
Large open – Wilton 199
Extra-large – Wilton 1M

OTHER TIPS

Grass/multi-opening decorating tip – Wilton 233
Leaf tip – Wilton 352
Basket-weave tip – Wilton 47

Piping tips can simply be placed inside the end of a piping bag with a small portion of the bag tip cut off, or they can be attached from the outside of a piping bag with a coupler.

COUPLERS

Using a coupler allows you to change tips midway through a bag of frosting.

To attach a coupler, insert the coupler base (ring removed) narrow end first into the bag and push it down to the end. Cut the tip off the bag just below the coupler. Push the coupler base down so that the end of the thread is showing at the cut opening. Place the piping tip over the outside and screw the coupler ring over the tip into place. You're ready to go!

Note

It is helpful to purchase multiple tips of the size and shape you use most often. This means you don't have to wash and dry the tips every time you want to change colors.

Piping Bags

For the cakes in this book I recommend using inexpensive disposable piping bags, which are available at supermarkets, cake-decorating stores, and online. If you're absolutely stuck, you can use a zippered plastic bag with the piping tip fitted in one of the corners.

Some recipes do not call for a piping tip. In this case, simply cut a tiny portion off the bag tip and try piping. If the hole is too small, cut off some more, repeating until the desired width is achieved. It is always better to start with a hole that is too small!

Attach tips and couplers (if using) to the bag before adding the frosting. An easy way to fill a bag with frosting is to place the bag in a tall glass and fold the top part of the bag down over the edge of the glass. This not only keeps the mouth of the piping bag clean and holds it open, but it also provides a hard edge so you can scrape the frosting off your spatula. Once you have added the frosting to the bag, fold up the top edges of the bag and remove it from the glass. Squeeze any air pockets out of the bag before you tightly twist the top (you don't want any surprise air pockets exploding out of the tip while you are piping).

I find it easier to hold a half-full piping bag and refill it rather than trying to pipe with a bag that is ready to burst.

KNIT PATTERN (WINTER BEANIE, PAGE 147)

1. Fit a medium petal tip (Wilton 104) to a piping bag. Fill the bag with frosting. Hold with the wide opening of the petal tip facing upward. To make the first "stitch," begin at the top of the cake and pipe a ½ inch diagonal line. Pipe a second line on the opposite diagonal to make a V shape. Repeat, piping diagonal lines to make a zigzag stitch around the cake.

ROSETTES (#7, PAGE 199)

1. Fit an extra-large star tip (Wilton 1M) to a piping bag. Fill the bag with frosting. Squeeze out a blob of frosting to form the center of the rosette.

2. Without releasing pressure and while squeezing consistently, pipe in a circular motion around the center.

2. With your second frosting color, repeat the zigzag pattern directly below (but slightly overlapping) the first row.

3. Pipe the next row with the third color.

4. Pipe the next row with fourth color, and so on.

3. When close to completing the circle, decrease the pressure and let the frosting thin out as you complete the rotation.

4. Release the pressure, complete circle motion, and pull the bag away so the tail of the frosting follows the circle.

TUTU SKIRT (THE DANCING TUTU CUPCAKES, PAGE 105)

1. Fit a medium petal tip (Wilton 104) to a piping bag. Fill the bag with frosting. Hold the tip at a 45-degree angle with the wide opening of the petal tip facing up.

2. Pipe a long strip all the way out to the edge of the cupcake and back to the center in a continuous motion.

WAVES (TREASURE ISLAND, PAGE 94)

1. Fit a large open star tip (Wilton 199) to a piping bag. Fill the bag with frosting. Squeezing consistently, pipe a curl in a counterclockwise motion.

2. Without releasing the pressure, continue the curl to make an S shape.

3. Repeat, slightly overlapping the previous petal.

4. Continue the pattern around the cupcake in a circular motion to complete the tutu.

3. Form the next curl so that it overlaps the tail of the previous curl, this time beginning in a clockwise motion and finishing in a counterclockwise motion. Continue the pattern around the cake, piping alternating clockwise and counterclockwise curls.

4. Start the next row below the first, beginning the pattern in the trough of the wave above.

BASKET WEAVE (UP, UP & AWAY, PAGE 116)

1. Fit a basket-weave tip (Wilton 47) to a piping bag. Fill the bag with frosting. Hold the tip with the serrated edge facing up. Pipe a vertical line from the top to the bottom edge of the cake.

2. Pipe 1¼ inch long horizontal lines over the vertical line. The spacing between the horizontal lines should be equal to the width of the tip.

ROPE (UP, UP & AWAY, PAGE 116)

1. Fit a medium round tip (Wilton 4) to a piping bag and fill the bag with frosting. Squeezing consistently, pipe an S shape on the edge of the cake.

2. Start the next S shape under the curve of the first S, then pipe up and over the tail.

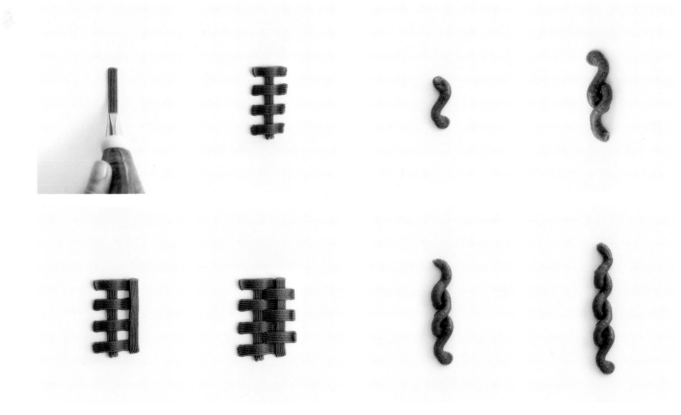

3. Pipe a second vertical line overlapping the ends of the horizontal lines.

4. Starting with the tip against the first vertical line, pipe the next row of 1¼ inch horizontal lines, fitting them snugly into the gaps. Continue this pattern around the cake.

3. Repeat the pattern.

4. Continue the rope pattern around the cake, completing the circle by tucking the tail of the final S in the curve of the first.

FLOWERS (THE FLOWERPOT, PAGE 173)

1. Fit a small petal tip (Wilton 102) to a piping bag. Fill the bag with royal icing. Hold the tip parallel to your work surface, with the narrow end of the petal tip facing out and the wide end toward where the center of your flower will be. Pipe 2 petals side-by-side in an M-shaped motion. The 2 petals should be about 1 inch wide when completed.

2. Using the same motion, pipe 2 slightly smaller petals overlapping the first set.

LEAVES (THE FLOWERPOT, PAGE 173)

1. Fit a leaf tip (Wilton 352) to a piping bag. Fill the bag with alternating heaped spoonfuls of 2 shades of green royal icing. Hold the piping tip almost parallel to the work surface, with the opening vertical. Firmly squeeze out the royal icing to create the base of the leaf.

2. Without releasing pressure and while squeezing consistently, wiggle the tip backward and forward while drawing the bag toward you.

3. Change to a second piping bag filled with your second royal icing color and fitted with a small petal tip (Wilton 102). Using the same technique as above, pipe 3 small petals to complete the other half of the flower.

4. Fit a small round tip (Wilton 3) to a third piping bag filled with yellow royal icing and pipe a yellow circle in the center of each flower.

3. Each wiggle will create a ridge on the leaf. Decrease the pressure of each wiggle as you taper the leaf.

4. At the end of your leaf, release the pressure and pull away to create a point.

WHY
I ♡ USA
CUPCAKES

TECHNIQUES

Melting chocolate, page 19
Rolling out fondant, page 21
Creating a smooth finish, page 18

STENCILS

Side C: Why I ♡ USA Cupcakes (eagle head, surfer, cowboy hat & Route 66)

WHAT YOU NEED

9 cupcakes (see recipes, pages 12–13)
1 quantity buttercream (see recipe, page 20)
fondant: 5 oz white, 1 oz yellow, 2 oz red, 2 oz light brown, 2 oz chocolate brown & 1 oz blue
gel food coloring: black, yellow, mint green & red
2 oz white chocolate
5 white sprinkle stars
2 white sprinkle hearts
7 candy corn candies
1 milk chocolate disk
1 x 3-oz package blue Jell-O
cornstarch, for rolling out fondant
9 white cupcake liners
1 toothpick
1 small paintbrush or black edible-ink pen
1 rolling pin

INSTRUCTIONS

Bake the cupcakes in the liners and leave them to cool completely. Make the buttercream.

To make the USA cupcake toppers, trace and cut out the stencils for the eagle head, cowboy hat, and Route 66.

EAGLE: Thinly roll out the white fondant to a thickness of ⅛ inch, place your eagle head stencil on top, and cut out the shape. Thinly roll out the yellow fondant and cut a ¼-inch oval, which is pointed at each end, for the eye. Place the eagle beak part of your stencil on the remaining yellow fondant and cut out a beak shape. Use a little water to stick the eye and beak to the white fondant head. Using the black edible-ink pen or the small paintbrush dipped in black gel food coloring, carefully color in the eye leaving a thin strip of yellow fondant along the bottom uncolored, and paint the black outlines around the head, beak, and eye, as shown.

I ♡ NY: Thinly roll out white fondant to a thickness of ⅛ inch and cut out a circle 1¼ inches in diameter. Thinly roll out red fondant and cut out a ½-inch heart shape. Stick the heart on the top right corner of the white circle with a little water. Using the black edible-ink pen or the small paintbrush dipped in black gel food coloring, write the words "I" and "NY" on the white circle.

BASEBALL GLOVE & BALL: Mold the light brown fondant into a round disk measuring 1¼ inch in diameter. Using the back of the paintbrush, press in 1 thick groove to separate the thumb, as shown, and then make 3 half cuts next to this to make the fingers. Roll a pea-sized ball of white fondant into a sphere. Roll a thin rope of red fondant measuring 1¼-inch long and use a little water to stick it to the white ball of fondant, as shown. Stick the ball into the center of the glove with a little water.

FIREWORKS: Thinly roll out white fondant to a thickness of ⅛ inch and cut out a circle 1¼ inch in diameter. Using the small paintbrush dipped in yellow food coloring, draw a burst on one edge of the circle, as shown. Repeat with the mint green and red food coloring, washing the brush in between colors.

Why I Love USA Cupcakes continues on page 36 . . .

WHY
I ♥ USA
CUPCAKES

CONTINUED

FLAG: Thinly roll out white fondant to a thickness of ⅛ inch and cut out a 1½-by-2½-inch rectangle. Thinly roll out the blue fondant and cut out a ¾-by-1¼-inch rectangle. Use a little water to stick the blue rectangle on the top left corner of the white rectangle. Thinly roll out the red fondant, cut 3 strips measuring ¼ inch wide and 2½ inches long. Cut one of these strips in half. Use a little water to stick the red strips, evenly spaced, across the flag. Melt white chocolate and use a toothpick to stick the 5 white sprinkle stars on the blue rectangle.

SURFER: Thinly roll out white fondant to a thickness of ⅛ inch and cut out a circle 1¼ inch in diameter. Using the black edible-ink pen or the small paintbrush dipped in black gel food coloring, paint the surfer in the center of the circle, as shown, using the surfer stencil as a guide.

COWBOY HAT: Thinly roll out the chocolate brown fondant to a thickness of ⅛ inch, place the cowboy hat stencil on top, and cut out the entire hat to make a base layer. Now cut down your cowboy hat stencil into 3 pieces: the top, the band, and the upturned brim. Place the top of the hat and the upturned brim on the chocolate brown fondant and cut out the shapes. Thinly roll out the light brown fondant, place the band piece of your stencil on top and cut out the light brown band shape. Use a little water to stick the pieces of the hat onto the base layer.

ROUTE 66: Thinly roll out white fondant to a thickness of ⅛ inch, place the Route 66 stencil on top and cut out the shape. Using the black edible-ink pen or the small paintbrush dipped in black gel food coloring, outline the sign and paint a horizontal line across the narrowest part of it. Paint "ROUTE" above the horizontal line and "66" below the horizontal line.

TURKEY: Spoon a teaspoonful of melted white chocolate onto a piece of parchment paper and press in the 7 candy corn candies in a circular shape, as shown. Using more melted white chocolate, stick the milk chocolate disk in the center. Roll the remaining red fondant into 2 thin ropes measuring ½ inch long each. Thinly roll out the rest of the yellow fondant and cut out a small triangle. Use the melted white chocolate to stick the red fondant ropes under the yellow triangle and to the milk chocolate disk. Use the melted white chocolate to stick the white sprinkle hearts to the milk chocolate disk to make the eyes. Use the black edible-ink pen or paintbrush dipped in black food coloring to make a dot in each eye. Set the turkey topper aside to allow the white chocolate to harden.

Frost the cupcakes with buttercream to a smooth finish. Sprinkle blue Jell-O crystals in a semicircle on one of the cupcakes. Place a USA topper on each cupcake, with the surfer going on top of the cupcake decorated with Jell-O.

"THAT'S MY FAVORITE PLAYER" CAKE

WHAT YOU NEED

2 rectangular (9-by-13-inch) cakes (see recipes, pages 12–13)

1 quantity buttercream or ganache (see recipes, pages 20–21)

cornstarch, for rolling out fondant

fondant: 4 lb white, 13 oz blue, 3 oz black & 1¾ oz red

1 rolling pin

1 fondant smoother

1 toothpick

1 clean pen cap

1 ruler

TECHNIQUES

Leveling, page 18

Crumb coating, page 18

Rolling out fondant, page 21

Covering a cake with fondant, page 23

STENCILS

Side C: "That's My Favorite Player" Cake
(half baseball shirt, Y collar & sleeve)

INSTRUCTIONS

Bake the cakes. Turn them out and leave them to cool completely. Make the buttercream or ganache.

TO MAKE THE SHIRT: Trace the half baseball shirt stencil onto parchment paper and cut it out. Level the cakes and turn them over. Using your stencil, cut out a shoulder and then half a torso from one cake and then turn the stencil over and repeat with the second cake. Put the pieces of cake on a serving plate, arrange them into the shape of a shirt, then stick them together with buttercream or ganache. Crumb coat the cake with a thin layer of frosting and refrigerate it until dry to the touch. Roll out 3 lb of white fondant to a thickness of ¼ inch and a diameter of about 20 inches. Place the fondant over the cake, then smooth and trim it.

Knead together the blue and black fondant to make navy fondant. Trace the sleeve stencil onto parchment paper and cut it out. Roll out the navy fondant, place your stencil on top of the fondant, and cut out the sleeve shape. Place the fondant sleeve over one arm, then smooth and trim it. Turn the stencil over, then repeat this process to create the other sleeve.

Decide what number you would like on your shirt and then make your own stencil by either drawing it or printing it onto paper at a height of 3 inches. Cut out your stencil. Roll out navy fondant to a thickness of ⅛ inch, place your number stencil on top of the fondant, and cut out your number. Cut 1/16 inch off the edges of your paper number stencil. Roll out red fondant to a thickness of ⅛ inch, place your smaller number stencil on top of the fondant and cut out your number again. Stick the red number on top of the navy number with a little water. Set this aside on a piece of parchment paper.

"That's My Favorite Player" Cake continues on page 38 . . .

"THAT'S MY FAVORITE PLAYER" CAKE

CONTINUED

TO MAKE THE COLLAR: Trace the Y collar stencil onto parchment paper and cut it out. Roll out the white fondant to a thickness of ¼ inch, place your stencil on the fondant, and cut out the Y collar. Place the collar on the cake, as shown, sticking it down with a little water and trimming the ends. Use a knife to gently indent the edge of the shirt placket as shown on the stencil. Roll out the remaining white fondant to a thickness of ⅛ inch and use a pen cap or another round object of a similar size to punch out 6 small circles. Use the toothpick to prick 4 holes in the top of each circle to make the buttons. Evenly space the buttons down the Y collar, sticking them on with a little water.

Roll out the navy fondant to a length measuring 24 inches long. Cut 2 long strips measuring ¼ inch wide and 24 inches long. Using a little water, stick the 2 lengths to the outer edge of the Y collar, as shown.

TO MAKE THE STRIPES: Roll out the remaining navy fondant to a thickness of ⅛ inch and, using a ruler, cut 8 long, thin strips 24 inches long and only 1/16 inch wide (as thin as you can without the fondant breaking when it's lifted). Carefully roll up one stripe at a time around a rolling pin or similar and then unroll it vertically over the shirt and down the top and bottom edges. Once all the stripes are evenly spaced over the shirt, trim the tops of the 2 middle stripes to show the inside of the shirt, trim around the number, trim the thin stripes overlapping the thick strips, and trim the ends where the cake meets the serving plate. Stick the ends of the stripes down with a little water if necessary to stop them from moving.

Note
Make the shirt in your favorite team's colors, or change the number to your favorite player's number or the age of the birthday person!

TOUCHDOWN!

TECHNIQUES

Creating a smooth finish, page 18; Rolling out fondant, page 21; Covering a cake with fondant, page 23; Coloring, page 24; Leveling, page 18

INSTRUCTIONS

Bake the cake. Turn it out and leave it to cool completely.

TO MAKE THE KICKING TEE: Knead black fondant, then mold it into a U shape measuring 5 inches long and 3 inches wide. Bend the arms of the U upward on a right angle to create a cradle for the ball. Insert a skewer vertically into each arm and set the kicking tee aside.

TO MAKE THE FOOTBALL: Make the Rice Krispies Treats. As soon as the mixture is cool enough to touch, spray cooking oil on your hands and tightly press the mixture into an oval shape that is slightly pointed at each end. Set the Rice Krispies Treats ball aside to cool and harden, then use a serrated knife to carve off any irregularities so that the ball is symmetrical.

Make the buttercream, then thickly spread it all over the ball to a smooth finish. Knead the red and brown fondant together with your hands to make the football color. Roll out this fondant to a thickness of ¼ inch and a rectangle of approximately 10 by 12 inches. Lay the fondant over the Rice Krispies Treats ball and use your fingers to smooth the fondant around the ball. Use a sharp knife to cut off any excess fondant, pressing the edges together neatly on the underside of the ball. Use a knife to gently indent 4 seam lines lengthwise down the ball at evenly spaced intervals, as shown. Thinly roll out white fondant and cut out 2 rectangles, each measuring ¾ by 6 inches. Wrap the rectangles around the ball and trim the ends at the side seam lines. Use a knife to gently indent the seam lines on the white fondant to match the existing seam lines on the ball.

WHAT YOU NEED

1 rectangular (9-by-13-inch) chocolate cake (see recipe, page 13)
fondant: 7 oz black, 9 oz red, 9 oz brown/chocolate & 5 oz white
Rice Krispies Treats (9 cups Rice Krispies
  & 4½ cups mini marshmallows; see recipe, page 14)
½ quantity buttercream (see recipe, page 20)
1 quantity royal icing (see recipe, page 20)
gel food coloring: black & green
cooking spray, for molding Rice Krispies Treats
cornstarch, for rolling out fondant
3 skewers
2 piping bags
1 small round tip (Wilton 3)
1 grass tip (Wilton 233)
1 ruler
1 rolling pin

STENCIL

Side C: Touchdown!
(football stitching)

Trace the football stitching stencil onto parchment paper and cut it out. Place your stencil on top of the ball and gently indent the outline and the stitch holes with a skewer.

To make the laces, roll out white fondant to a thickness of ⅛ inch, and using a ruler cut 2 strips ¼ by 3½ inches. Place these 2 lacing strips inside the stitching outline, along either side of the seam line. Cut 8 strips of white fondant measuring ¼ by 1 inch and pinch the ends of each. Place the strips across the long laces, poking the pinched ends down into the stitch holes.

Prepare the royal icing, put 2 tablespoons into a bowl, and set aside the rest, covering it with plastic wrap to prevent it from drying out. Color the 2 tablespoons of icing black, fit the small round tip to a piping bag, and fill it with the black icing. Carefully pipe over the previously indented outline.

TO MAKE THE FIELD: Level the cake and turn it over. Place the cake on a serving plate. Color half of the remaining royal icing light green and the other half dark green. Cover the bowls of icing with plastic wrap to prevent them from drying out. Fit the grass tip to a new piping bag and fill the bag with one shade of green icing. Randomly pipe blobs of icing while pulling up and away from the cake, leaving gaps for the second shade of green. Refill the piping bag with the second shade of green and fill in the gaps. It's fine if you don't cover the cake completely, as the chocolate cake peeking through looks like dirt on the field.

Place the tee on the cake and push the skewers down through the tee and into the cake. Place the ball on the tee, inserting the top end of the skewers into the underside of the ball for support.

SWOOSH!

WHAT YOU NEED

1 chocolate hemisphere cake (see recipe, page 13)
½ quantity buttercream or ganache (see recipes, pages 20–21)
fondant: 19 oz orange & 7 oz black
cornstarch, for rolling out fondant
1 ruler
1 cheese grater
1 rolling pin

TECHNIQUES

Creating a smooth finish, page 18
Covering a cake with fondant, page 23

INSTRUCTIONS

Bake the cake. Turn it out and leave it to cool completely.

Make the buttercream or ganache.

Once the cake is cool, put it back in the hemisphere pan and use a serrated knife to cut any uneven rising off the cake to level it. Turn the cake out and place it on a serving plate.

TO COVER THE BALL: Frost the cake with buttercream or ganache to a smooth finish. Knead all the orange and ½ oz of the black fondant together with your hands to make the basketball color. Roll out the fondant to a thickness of ¼ inch and a diameter of 10 inches. Place the fondant over the cake, then smooth and trim it.

Make the grip pattern on the surface of the ball by gently pressing the cheese grater, using the side with the smallest holes, into the fondant using a rolling motion from front to back.

TO MAKE THE BLACK LINES: Roll out the remaining 6½ oz black fondant and cut 4 lengths measuring ¼ by 12 inches. Using a little water, stick one of the lengths across the middle of the ball. Cut a ¼-inch gap in the center of this black length. Measure 1 inch along from this gap and cut another ¼-inch gap. Repeat on the other side of the center line.

Using a little water, stick the second length of black fondant across the middle, through the middle gap, to create an X shape. Using a little water, stick another fondant length in an upside down U shape on the side of the ball, as shown. Repeat with the final length of black fondant on the opposite side.

Make a Splash

WHAT YOU NEED

1 rectangular (9-by-13-inch) cake
   (see recipes, pages 12–13)

1 x 3-oz package blue Jell-O

62 oz white chocolate in bars
   or mini white chocolate Kit Kat bars,
   plus 2 oz white chocolate for melting

1 quantity white chocolate ganache
   (see recipe, page 21)

5 x 8-inch (approx.) licorice laces

2 rainbow belt candies

3 white Jordan almonds

3 M&M's or similar round candy-coated chocolate candies

3 twisted pretzels

6 straight pretzels

1 candy necklace

4 x 8-inch-lengths floral wire

4 skewers

4 straws

TECHNIQUES

Melting chocolate, page 19
Leveling, page 18

INSTRUCTIONS

Bake the cake. Turn it out and leave it to cool completely. Make the ganache and set it aside to firm up.

Make the Jell-O on the day you intend to serve the cake. Mix it up according to the packet's instructions and put it in the fridge to set until the Jell-O is the consistency of egg whites (2 hours approximately).

Break the bars of chocolate into individual pieces and trim off any messy edges. Save the messy edges for melting later.

Level the cake, then use a serrated knife and a spoon to cut and scoop out a ¾-inch-deep rectangle pool with a ¾-inch-thick border all around the edge of it.

Thickly coat the cake in ganache, including the inside of the pool, then stick the chocolate pieces all over the cake (excluding the inside of the pool) in a brick pattern.

TO MAKE THE BLACK LANE MARKERS ON THE POOL BOTTOM: Lay 3 evenly spaced licorice laces down the length of the pool. Cut the 2 remaining licorice laces into thirds and place one at each end of the long licorice laces to make an I shape.

TO MAKE THE FLAGS: Use a sharp knife to cut a zigzag pattern into a rainbow belt candy. Take a piece of wire and wrap each end of it around the tip of a skewer. Melt the white chocolate offcuts and use the melted chocolate to stick the flag ends to the wire. Repeat this process with the second rainbow belt candy. When the chocolate is dry, slide the straws over the skewers. Push the ends of the skewers into the cake, between the bricks, so that the flags span both sides of the pool.

Once the Jell-O has reached egg-white consistency, pour it into the pool. Once you have added the Jell-O, the cake will need to be kept in the fridge until serving.

Just before serving, add the swimmers and the lane dividers to the Jell-O (if you add them too early, they will dissolve in the Jell-O).

TO MAKE THE SWIMMERS: Place a white Jordan almond in the Jell-O over each of the licorice lane markers. Put 2 straight pretzels at the bottom of each body for legs. Cut the twisted pretzel pieces in half and place a curved piece on the sides of each body for arms. Add a candy-coated chocolate candy head at the end of each body.

TO MAKE THE LANE DIVIDERS: Cut open the candy necklace and thread half the candies onto a piece of wire and the other half onto another. Position the lane dividers between the swimmers and insert the wire ends into the cake at each end of the pool.

KICKED-a-GOAL!

1 chocolate hemisphere cake (see recipe, page 13)
½ quantity buttercream (see recipe, page 20)
2 quantities royal icing (see recipe, page 20)
gel food coloring: black & green
Rice Krispies Treats (7 cups Rice Krispies &
   3½ cups mini marshmallows; see recipe, page 14)
cooking spray, for molding Rice Krispies Treats

3 piping bags
1 grass tip (Wilton 233)
2 small star tips (Wilton 30)
1 medium round tip (Wilton 4)
sewing pins
1 round (8-inch) cake board or plate

TECHNIQUES

Crumb coating, page 18
Coloring, page 24

STENCILS

Side D: Kicked-a-Goal! (hexagon & pentagon)

INSTRUCTIONS

Bake the cake. Turn it out and leave it to cool completely. Once cooled, place the hemisphere cake back in the pan and use a serrated knife to cut off any uneven rising to level it. Turn the cake out and stand it up the right way.

TO MAKE THE BOTTOM HALF OF THE BALL: Thickly spray the hemisphere pan with cooking spray. Make the Rice Krispies Treats. As soon as the mixture is cool enough to touch, spray cooking oil on your hands and press it tightly into the hemisphere pan. Set the pan of Rice Krispies Treats aside to cool and harden.

Turn the hardened Rice Krispies Treats out of the hemisphere pan. Using a sharp serrated knife, cut a flat spot about 3 inches wide at the top of the dome. This will provide a stable balancing point for the ball. Make the buttercream. Cover the 8-inch flat surface of the Rice Krispies Treats with buttercream and place the dome cake on top to create a ball shape. Trim the edges to match.

Crumb coat the ball with a thin layer of the buttercream, then refrigerate it until dry to the touch.

Make the royal icing and divide it evenly among 3 bowls. Color 1 bowl black, 1 bowl green, and leave the third bowl uncolored. Cover the bowls with plastic wrap to prevent the icing from drying out.

TO MAKE THE GRASS: Fit the grass tip to a piping bag and fill the bag with green icing. Pipe blobs of icing onto the cake board or serving plate while pulling up and away from the cake. Pipe the tufts of grass close together so that the surface underneath is completely covered.

Once the ball cake is dry to the touch, stick it to the green royal icing in the middle of the grassy board or plate.

TO MAKE THE PATTERN ON THE BALL: Trace the pentagon and hexagon stencils onto parchment paper and cut them out. Label the stencils. Fit a medium round tip to a new piping bag and fill the bag with black royal icing. Pin the pentagon cutout on the top of the ball, then outline it in black royal icing. Pin the hexagon cutout edge to edge against 1 side of the pentagon, then outline the hexagon in black royal icing. Repeat this process, moving the hexagon stencil around all 5 sides of the pentagon until you have piped 5 hexagon outlines.

When the top pentagon is surrounded with hexagons on all sides, move the pentagon stencil and pin it between 2 hexagons, as shown. Pipe pentagon outlines in the gaps created by the hexagon row above. Continue this pentagon and hexagon row pattern all the way down the ball. Refer to the picture or a real soccer ball to make sure you have the right pattern. Change to a star tip and pipe small star-shaped dots to completely fill in each pentagon with black royal icing.

Fit the star tip to a new piping bag and fill the bag with white royal icing. Pipe small star dots to completely fill in each hexagon in the white royal icing, making sure the black outlines are still visible.

Note
Use gel color when coloring royal icing black, as liquid coloring will make the icing too runny.

INTO THE
WILD

WHAT YOU NEED

1 x 3-oz package blue Jell-O

2 rectangular-shaped crackers

3 ice cream sugar cones (see page 19)

1 quantity royal icing (see recipe, page 20)

1 rectangular (9-by-13-inch) chocolate cake
  (see recipe, page 13)

1 quantity buttercream (see recipe, page 20)

food coloring: blue

gel food coloring: green

3½ cups shredded coconut

15 (approx.) straight pretzels

1 large zippered plastic bag

1 piping bag

1 small star tip (Wilton 30)

8 (approx.) red, orange & yellow candles

TECHNIQUES

Coloring, page 24

Coloring coconut, page 19

Leveling, page 18

INSTRUCTIONS

Make Jell-O, tent, and trees at least a day in advance to allow for drying time.

Make blue Jell-O according to packet instructions, pour it into a shallow baking pan, and refrigerate until set.

TO MAKE THE TENT: Make royal icing. Lean the crackers together and use white royal icing to glue the apex of the tent together. Set tent aside on parchment paper to dry.

TO MAKE THE TREES: Divide the remaining royal icing into 2 bowls and color one green and the other dark green. Using a serrated knife, trim the wide end off 2 of the ice cream sugar cones to create 3 trees of different heights. Fit the star tip to the piping bag and half fill it with one green icing. Randomly pipe icing over all 3 trees, leaving gaps for the second color. Refill the piping bag with the second color and fill in all the remaining gaps on the cones. Set the cones aside to dry, standing them upright on a piece of parchment paper. Store the tent and trees in an airtight container for up to a week.

Color coconut green for the grass.

Bake the cake, turn it out, and leave it to cool completely. Make the buttercream. Color 3 heaped tablespoons light blue and set aside. Color the remaining buttercream green.

Level the cake, turn it over, and cut it into a square. Save the offcut piece for crumbling into dirt under the campfire. Place the square cake on the serving dish. Cover the cake's top and sides in green buttercream and immediately pour over the green coconut grass, pressing it into the buttercream. Shake off any excess coconut.

TO MAKE THE CAMPFIRE: In the front left corner of the cake, crumble some cake offcut in a small circle to look like dirt. Push 4 or 5 different-colored candles into the center of the crumbs and arrange the straight pretzels around them as firewood, using leftover royal icing to glue them in place.

Place the tent behind the fire and add a straight pretzel at each end of it for tent poles, inserting them into the cake. At the front right-hand side of the cake, use a serrated knife to carve out a winding river shape ½ inch deep by 1½ inches wide. Spread blue buttercream over the bottom and sides of the river. Arrange the cone trees around the river. Just before serving the cake, take the Jell-O out of the fridge and spoon it over the blue buttercream. Refrigerate the cake until serving.

INSTRUCTIONS

Make the ganache and set it aside to firm up.

Bake the cake. Turn it out and leave it to cool completely.

Trace wing, spike, and breast stencils onto paper and cut them out.

TO MAKE THE HAIR SPIKE: Place your spike stencil on a pink wafer and use the point of a sharp knife to cut out the spike shape. Set the spike aside.

TO MAKE THE WINGS: Place your wing stencil on a pink wafer and cut out the wing shape. Turn your stencil over and repeat to create a second wing. Pour chocolate sprinkles into a bowl. Cover one side of each wing in chocolate ganache and then press the wings into the bowl of chocolate sprinkles until covered. Set the wings aside.

TO MAKE THE RED BREAST: Place your breast stencil on a pink wafer and cut out the breast shape. Color coconut red and pour it into a bowl. Melt white chocolate. Cover the breast in melted white chocolate, then press it into the bowl of red coconut until it is well covered on one side. Set the breast aside on parchment paper to set.

TO MAKE THE EYES: Trace the eyes stencil onto a large piece of parchment paper, then lay the parchment paper flat on top of a baking sheet. Spoon melted white chocolate into the middle of the stencil, carefully spread chocolate to the edges of the stencil using a skewer, and place in the refrigerator until the chocolate is set.

Level the cake, turn it over, and attach it to the cake board with a little ganache. Cover the entire cake with ganache. Press the pink wafer spike into the ganache at the top of the cake and cover it with ganache. Place a bowl upside down in the middle of a shallow roasting pan and place the cake on top. Have fun with this part because it gets messy! Take small handfuls of chocolate sprinkles and press them into the sticky ganache with your fingers until the robin is completely covered. Place the cake on a serving plate. Attach the wings and red breast using a little chocolate ganache.

Once the chocolate eyes are completely set, remove them from the refrigerator, carefully peel away the parchment paper, and turn the eyes upside down so that the flat surface is facing upward. Separate the layers of the giant licorice allsort. Use the round cutter to cut 2 circles measuring ¾ inch each from the licorice layers, then stick them in place on the eyes using a little melted chocolate. Attach the eyes to the head with a little ganache. Use a skewer dipped in melted white chocolate to add whites to the eyes. Secure the yellow airplane-shaped gummy candy beak in position with a little ganache.

TO MAKE THE FEET: Push one end of a toothpick into the tip of each orange airplane-shaped gummy candy. Insert the feet into the cake.

Rockin' ROBIN

WHAT YOU NEED

1 quantity milk chocolate ganache (see recipe, page 21)
1 round (8-inch) chocolate cake (see recipe, page 13)
¼ cup shredded coconut
4 pink sugar wafers
1¾ cups chocolate sprinkles
food coloring: red
7 oz white chocolate
1 giant licorice allsort
3 airplane-shaped gummy candies: 2 orange & 1 yellow
1 large zippered plastic bag
2 skewers
1 round (8-inch) cake board
1 small round cookie cutter (¾-inch diameter)
2 toothpicks

TECHNIQUES

Cutting sugar wafers, page 19
Melting chocolate, page 19
Coloring coconut, page 19
Leveling, page 18

STENCILS

Side C: Rockin' Robin
(wing, spike, breast & eyes)

LUCY THE *Ladybug* IN *Sunflower Meadow*

WHAT YOU NEED

1 chocolate hemisphere cake (see recipe, page 13)
2 quantities royal icing (see recipe, page 20)
gel food colorings: black & red
2 round red candy-coated round chocolate candies
2 piping bags
2 medium round tips (Wilton 4)
1 round (8-inch) cake board
toothpicks
1 paintbrush
2 skewers
1 small glass

TECHNIQUE

Coloring, page 24

INSTRUCTIONS

Decorate this cake at least a day in advance to allow for drying time.

Bake the cake. Turn it out and leave it to cool completely. Once the cake is cool, put it back in the pan and use a sharp serrated knife to cut any uneven rising off the cake to level it. Turn the cake out.

Make the royal icing and set aside 2 heaped tablespoons in a small bowl. Equally divide the remaining royal icing between bowls and color one red and the other black. Cover the bowls with plastic wrap to prevent the royal icing from drying out.

Stick the cake to the cake board using a little black royal icing. Place the cake and board on an upside-down bowl with a pan underneath it to catch the drips. Spread the black royal icing over the half sphere, letting the excess icing drip off the bottom of the cake. Set the cake aside to dry (this could take 6–8 hours, depending on the humidity).

TO OUTLINE THE WINGS: When the black royal icing on the cake is dry to the touch (it's okay if it is still soft underneath), fit a medium round tip to a piping bag and fill the bag with a couple of tablespoons of red royal icing. Keep the remaining royal icing covered.

Pipe a thin red line two-thirds of the way across the sphere to separate the face and body, leaving a ½-inch gap in the middle of this line, as shown. Then, leaving a ½-inch gap all the way from front to back, pipe 2 lines along the top of the sphere to make the wings, as shown. To make the 3 spots on each wing, gently press the rim of a small glass onto the black icing. Remove the glass and pipe 3 large red outlines over the resulting imprints. Cover the wings with red icing, carefully going around the spots (you can use a toothpick to spread the icing). Allow any excess icing to drip off the bottom. Leave to dry.

TO MAKE THE ANTENNAE: Use the paintbrush to paint the 2 skewers with black food coloring and allow them to dry. Use the tip of a sharp knife to carefully "drill" a small hole in each red candy-coated chocolate candy and push the sharp end of the skewers into them.

When the red royal icing is dry enough, place the cake on the serving plate.

TO ADD THE EYES: Fit the second piping bag with a medium round tip and fill the bag with the reserved white royal icing. Using the glass-imprinting technique described above for the wings, pipe 3 white circles inside each other for each eye. Fill the smallest center circles and the outer ring with white icing, as shown, using a toothpick to spread the icing evenly inside the lines. Exactly where you place the pupils in the eyes is what gives the ladybug personality, so you may like to practice on paper first before adding the eyes to the cake. Insert the red candy-coated chocolate candy antennae into the cake above the eyes, at the top of the face.

Sunflower Meadow Cupcakes continues on page 54 . . .

Sunflower Meadow Cupcakes

TECHNIQUES

Coloring, page 24
Leveling, page 18

WHAT YOU NEED

½ quantity dark chocolate ganache
  (see recipe, page 21)
12 cupcakes (see recipes, pages 12–13)
½ quantity buttercream (see recipe, page 20)
food coloring: yellow
12 Oreo cookies
1 piping bag
1 leaf tip (Wilton 352)
1 palette knife
24 green cupcake liners

INSTRUCTIONS

Make the ganache and set it aside to firm up.

Bake 12 cupcakes in green cupcake wrappers and leave them to cool completely.

Make the buttercream and color it yellow. Fit the leaf tip to the piping bag and fill the bag with yellow buttercream. Set the bag aside.

Level the cupcakes.

Using a palette knife, frost the top of the cupcakes with ganache, then press an Oreo in the center of each.

TO PIPE THE YELLOW PETALS: Hold the piping bag upright so that the opening of the leaf tip is vertical and pipe ½-inch-long petals around the edge of each Oreo. Repeat for a second layer of petals.

To serve, place the cupcakes in a second green cupcake wrapper to create the stem of the plant below each flower.

TECHNIQUES

Coloring, page 24
Leveling, page 18
Stacking & filling, page 18
Melting chocolate, page 19
Crumb coating, page 18
Creating a smooth finish, page 18

WHAT YOU NEED

1 hemisphere cake (see recipes, pages 12–13)
1 round (8-inch) cake (see recipes, pages 12–13)
2 quantities buttercream (see recipe, page 20)
food coloring: yellow & red
3½ oz white chocolate
Rice Krispies Treats (17 cups Rice Krispies
  & 8½ cups mini marshmallows; see recipe,
  page 14)
1 box Froot Loops
1 giant licorice allsort
cooking spray, for molding Rice Krispies Treats
1 skewer
8 toothpicks
1 small round cookie cutter (¾ inch diameter)

STENCIL

Side C: Otto the Octopus (eyes)

INSTRUCTIONS

Bake the cakes. Turn them out and leave them to cool completely.

Make the buttercream and color it orange.

TO MAKE THE HEAD: Level the round cake. Place the hemisphere cake back in the pan and use a serrated knife to cut any uneven rising off the bottom of the cake to level it. Stack and fill the hemisphere cake on top of the round cake with buttercream. Trim off any overhang from the hemisphere cake so it matches the round cake below.

TO MAKE THE EYES: Trace the eyes stencil onto a large piece of parchment paper, then lay the parchment paper flat on top of a baking sheet. Melt the white chocolate, then spoon it into the middle of the stencil (leaving a little aside for sticking the eyes on later). Carefully use a skewer to spread chocolate to the edges of the stencil, then place the baking sheet in the refrigerator until the chocolate is set.

TO MAKE THE TENTACLES: Make the Rice Krispies Treats using 4¼ oz Rice Krispies and 4¼ oz marshmallows. As soon as the mixture is cool enough to touch, spray cooking oil on your hands, divide the mixture into 2 equal portions, and form 2 tentacles. Repeat this process 4 times to make 8 tentacles, all of varying shapes—curling up, down, and sideways, as shown on the next page. Set the tentacles aside to cool and harden.

Crumb coat the cake and tentacles with a thin layer of buttercream, then refrigerate them until dry to the touch. Place the cake in the center of a large serving plate and arrange the tentacles as desired, inserting one end of a toothpick into each tentacle and the other end into the cake to hold them in place.

Cover the entire cake and tentacles with buttercream to a smooth finish. Stick 2 rows of alternating green and purple Froot Loops to the buttercream on the underside of each tentacle, as shown.

Once the chocolate eyes are completely set, remove them from the refrigerator, carefully peel off the parchment paper, and turn the eyes upside down so that the flat surface is facing upward. Separate the layers of the giant licorice allsort. Use the round cutter to cut 2 circles measuring ¾ inch each from the licorice layers, then stick them in place on the chocolate eyes using a little melted chocolate. Attach the eyes to the head with a little buttercream or melted chocolate.

GRIZZ the Brown Bear

STENCILS

Side D: Grizz the Brown Bear
(kerchief, kerchief ties & mouth)

TECHNIQUES

Melting chocolate, page 19
Leveling, page 18
Rolling out fondant, page 21

WHAT YOU NEED

1 chocolate princess cake (see recipe, page 13)
1 quantity dark chocolate ganache (see recipe, page 21)
Rice Krispies Treats (9 cups Rice Krispies & 4½ cups
      mini marshmallows; see recipe, page 14)
7 oz white chocolate
9 cups Cocoa Krispies
12 chocolate-covered raisins
2 Mallomars
1 solid licorice stick
1 white marshmallow
1 licorice sheet
fondant: 3½ oz red, 2 oz white
cooking spray, for molding Rice Krispies Treats
1 skewer
2 toothpicks
1 piping bag
1 small round cookie cutter (¾ inch diameter)
1 rolling pin

INSTRUCTIONS

Make the ganache and set it aside to firm up.

Bake the cake. Turn it out and leave it to cool completely.

TO MAKE THE HEAD: Make the Rice Krispies Treats using 5 cups Rice Krispies and 3½ cups marshmallows. As soon as the mixture is cool enough to touch, spray cooking oil on your hands and tightly mold the mixture into a ball shape with a snout. Set this aside to cool and harden. Once the Rice Krispies Treats head is hard, melt the white chocolate and dip the snout into the white chocolate until covered, then set it aside to harden.

TO MAKE THE ARMS AND LEGS: Repeat the Rice Krispies Treats recipe, this time using 4 cups Rice Krispies and 2½ cups marshmallows. Divide the mixture into 4 equal parts and form them into teardrop shapes. Set the shapes aside on parchment paper to cool and harden.

TO MAKE THE TORSO: Place the cake back in the pan and use a sharp serrated knife to cut any uneven rising off the base of the cake to level it. Turn the cake out and place it upright. Using a sharp serrated knife, carve the bottom edge of the cake so it is rounded underneath to create a tummy shape. Place the torso on a serving plate. Stick one end of the skewer into the underside of the Rice Krispies Treats head and the other end into the middle of the cake so that the head sits on the torso. Attach the arms to the torso using toothpicks and ganache. Use ganache to stick the cylinder legs to the front of the torso. Cover the entire cake, apart from the snout, with ganache. Have fun with this part, because it gets messy! Press handfuls of Cocoa Krispies into the sticky ganache with your fingers until the entire bear, apart from the snout area, is completely covered. Push chocolate-covered raisin claws into place on the bear's arms and legs.

TO MAKE THE EARS: Cut a slight curve out of each Mallomar to match the shape of the head. Stick the ears to each side of the bear's head using chocolate ganache.

TO MAKE THE EYES: Cut 2 thin slices off the licorice stick. Cut the marshmallow in half horizontally and stick one piece of the sliced licorice stick to each of the marshmallow halves. Fill the piping bag with the leftover ganache, cut a tiny portion off the tip of the bag, then pipe a small amount of ganache onto the back of the marshmallow eyes. Stick the eyes to the bear's head.

TO MAKE THE MOUTH AND NOSE: For the mouth, trace the mouth stencil onto parchment paper and cut out the shape. Place your stencil onto the licorice sheet and cut out the mouth. Pipe a tiny amount of melted white chocolate onto the underside of the mouth and stick it to the bear's snout.

For the nose, cut out an oval 1½ inch long from the licorice sheet and attach it above the mouth with melted chocolate or ganache.

TO MAKE THE KERCHIEF: Trace the kerchief and kerchief ties stencils onto parchment paper and cut them out. Thinly roll out red fondant to a thickness of ⅛ inch, place your stencils on top, and cut out the shapes. Thinly roll out white fondant and use the cookie cutter to cut out about 15 circles. Stick the white fondant circles to the red kerchief and kerchief ties, as shown, using a little water. Trim off any overhanging white fondant. Drape the kerchief around the bear's neck, arranging it so the fondant folds up to give it shape. Add the kerchief ties at one side of the bear's neck.

Buzzing with EXCITEMENT!

1 chocolate princess cake (see recipe, page 13)
2 quantities buttercream (see recipe, page 20)
food coloring: yellow
fondant: 2½ oz yellow, 1 oz black & 1 oz white
cornstarch, for rolling out fondant
7 x 8-inch-lengths white floral wire
1 piping bag
1 extra-large round tip (Wilton 1A)
1 skewer
1 rolling pin

TECHNIQUES

Crumb coating, page 18
Rolling out fondant, page 21

INSTRUCTIONS

Bake the cake. Turn it out and leave it to cool completely.

Make the buttercream and color it yellow.

Crumb coat the cake with a thin layer of buttercream, then refrigerate it until dry to the touch. Place the cake on the serving plate.

TO PIPE THE BEEHIVE: Fit the extra-large round tip to the piping bag and fill the bag with yellow buttercream. Starting at the base of the cake, pipe a full circle around the cake. Repeat, piping circles around the cake all the way to the top. Finish with a blob of piping at the top.

TO MAKE THE BEES: Divide yellow fondant into 7 equal parts (½ oz each), then roll them into oval-shaped bodies. Thinly roll out black fondant, then cut 7 lengths that are ¼ inch wide and wrap one around the width of each yellow body. Trim off the excess fondant and secure it to the body with a dot of water. Use a skewer to poke 2 small eyeholes at one end of each bee body and fill them with tiny rolled balls of black fondant. To make the stingers, separate the remaining black fondant into 7 equal-sized cone shapes. Stick one to the back of each body with a little water and mold each into a spike. To make the wings, thinly roll out the white fondant and punch out 14 small round circles about ½ inch in diameter (the open end of a piping tip works well). Pinch each circle to make a teardrop shape and stick 2 wings to the back of each bee, with the point of each teardrop together and facing forward.

Wind one end of each piece of floral wire around a pen 3–5 times, keeping the rest of the wire straight. Carefully push the curled end of the wire into the underbelly of each bee and insert the straight end deep into the cake for support.

Notes
Add the buzzy bees to the cake on the day you serve it to prevent the wire from flopping overnight.

Make sure the wire is inserted deeply into the cake to hold the weight of the bee.

Samantha The STUPENDOUS pussycat

WHAT YOU NEED

1 round (10-inch) cake (see recipes, pages 12–13)

3 pink sugar wafers

1 quantity royal icing (see recipe, page 20)

gel food colorings: black & green

2 quantities buttercream (see recipe, page 20)

3 black licorice laces

1 large licorice allsort

1 small heart-shaped cutter

4 piping bags

3 medium round tips (Wilton 4) or use 1 tip and wash and dry it before changing colors

1 grass tip (Wilton 233)

STENCILS

Side C: Samantha the Stupendous Pussycat (ear, face, forehead & nose)

TECHNIQUES

Coloring, page 24

Leveling, page 18

Crumb coating, page 18

Royal icing (flood consistency), page 20

Cutting sugar wafers, page 19

INSTRUCTIONS

Bake the cake. Turn it out and leave it to cool completely.

TO MAKE THE EARS & NOSE: Trace the cat ear stencil onto paper and cut it out. Place your stencil on 2 of the pink sugar wafers and cut out 2 ears with the tip of a sharp knife. Using the heart-shaped cutter, punch a heart out of the remaining pink wafer.

Make the royal icing. Fill 2 bowls with 2 heaped tablespoons of royal icing each. Color 1 green and 1 black. Cover the bowls with plastic wrap to prevent the icing from drying out.

Make the buttercream and color it gray.

Level the cake, then crumb coat it with a thin layer of gray buttercream. Refrigerate the cake until dry to the touch.

TO MAKE THE FACE: Place the cake on a serving plate. Trace the cat face stencil onto paper, cut it out, and place it on the cake. Fit a medium round tip to a piping bag and fill it with 3 tablespoons of white royal icing. Using your stencil as a guide, pipe around the outline of the face, then pipe around the circle for the forehead and the circles for the cheeks, directly onto the cake. Set the piping bag aside. Once the piped outlines are dry to the touch, slowly add water to the bowl of leftover white royal icing until it reaches flood consistency. Spoon the icing inside the lines for the cat's forehead, nose, and mouth, and leave it to dry.

TO MAKE THE EYES: Fit a medium round tip to a new piping bag and add the green royal icing. Pipe the almond-shaped eyes with the green icing. Once the green icing has dried,

fit a medium round tip to another piping bag, add the black royal icing and pipe the black pupils on the eyes.

When the nose and mouth areas of the face are dry to the touch, fill in the cheeks with flood-consistency white royal icing. Filling these spaces separately will create definition in the cat's face.

Use the reserved piping bag of white royal icing to stick the wafer ears to the top of the cat's head, so that they stick out over the edge of the cake. Use royal icing to attach the heart-shaped wafer to the nose.

Whip the remaining gray buttercream again until it is light and fluffy. Attach the grass tip to the remaining piping bag and fill the bag with buttercream. Pipe blobs of frosting while pulling up and away from the cake. Pipe the clusters close together, ensuring the cake surface is not showing through. Take care to pipe carefully around the facial features and the edges of the ears.

TO MAKE THE MOUTH & WHISKERS: Cut the licorice laces in half to make 6 whiskers and stick them onto the cat's face using white royal icing. Peel apart the layers of the large licorice allsort and cut an anchor shape from one of the squares of licorice to form the cat's mouth. Stick the mouth on with white royal icing.

Finally, use the white royal icing to pipe a white spot in the pupil of each eye.

MURRAY
THE Sheep

WHAT YOU NEED

1 quantity milk chocolate ganache (see recipe, page 21)

17 oz milk chocolate

1 round (10-inch) cake (see recipes, pages 12–13)

12½ cups white marshmallows

2 chocolate chips

2 Twix chocolate bars

1 can cutter (see page 17)

4 skewers

TECHNIQUES

Creating a smooth finish, page 18

STENCIL

Side D: Murray the Sheep

INSTRUCTIONS

Make the ganache and set it aside to firm up.

TO MAKE THE HEAD: Trace the head stencil onto parchment paper. Instead of cutting it out, lay it flat on a baking sheet. Melt milk chocolate and spoon it into the middle of the stencil. Use your spoon to gently push the melted chocolate out to the edges of the stencil shape. Refrigerate the chocolate shape until set.

Bake the cake. Turn it out and leave it to cool completely.

Carefully holding the can cutter, place the can in the center of the cake's dome and push it down all the way through the cake to punch out the middle. Discard the cake center. Do not level the cake.

Cover the cake with ganache to a smooth finish. Fill the center hole with marshmallows and then press marshmallows into the ganache, completely covering the cake.

Once the chocolate head has set hard, remove it from the fridge and carefully peel it back from the parchment paper. Flip it over so that the flat side faces upward. Secure the head to the top of the cake with a little ganache.

TO MAKE THE EYES: Cut 1 marshmallow in half horizontally using scissors and attach the 2 sticky sides to the chocolate face. Attach chocolate chips to the eyes with a little ganache.

TO MAKE THE LEGS: Cut each Twix chocolate bar in half crosswise, push skewers into the cut ends, then push the skewers into the side of the cake.

WHAT YOU NEED

1 quantity milk chocolate ganache (see recipe, page 21)
1 rectangular (9-by-13-inch) cake
  (see recipes, pages 12–13)
1 quantity buttercream (see recipe, page 20)
food colorings: black, red & yellow
1 tbsp cocoa powder (optional)
3 piping bags
2 large round tips (Wilton 6)
1 extra-large star tip (Wilton 1M)

TECHNIQUES

Coloring, page 24
Leveling, page 18
Crumb coating, page 18
Creating a smooth finish, page 18

STENCIL

Side C: A Horse of Course!

A HORSE of course!

INSTRUCTIONS

Make the ganache and set it aside to firm up.

Bake the cake. Turn it out and leave it to cool completely.

Make the buttercream. Fit a piping bag with a large round tip and dollop 1 tablespoon of buttercream into it. Set the bag aside.

Color the remaining buttercream light brown, adding cocoa to deepen the color if necessary.

Level the cake and turn it over.

Trace the horse stencil onto parchment paper and cut it out. Place your stencil on the cake and cut out the horse shape. Place the cake on a serving plate.

Crumb coat the cake with a thin layer of light brown buttercream. Refrigerate the cake until dry to the touch, then cover the cake with light brown buttercream to a smooth finish.

Fit a large round tip to a piping bag (or just cut a tiny portion off the tip of the bag) and fill the bag with ganache. Pipe details for the horse's ears, eye, mouth, nose, and cheek, as shown.

Using the reserved bag of uncolored buttercream, pipe white details onto the horse's eye.

Fit the extra-large star tip to the last piping bag and fill it with ganache. Pipe long strips of ganache to form a shaggy mane, as shown.

STENCIL

Side B: Tim the Turkey

WHAT YOU NEED

1 quantity milk chocolate ganache (see recipe, page 21)
1 round (8-inch) cake (see recipes, pages 12–13)
5½ oz milk chocolate
5½ oz dark chocolate
1 white marshmallow
2 small chocolate chips
3 orange airplane-shaped gummy candies
1 red fruit roll-up
2 toothpicks

TECHNIQUES

Melting chocolate, page 19
Leveling, page 18

INSTRUCTIONS

Make the ganache and set it aside to firm up.

Bake the cake. Turn it out and leave it to cool completely.

TO MAKE THE TURKEY BODY: Trace the turkey stencil onto parchment paper, then lay the parchment paper flat on top of a baking sheet. Melt milk chocolate, then spoon it onto the outer edge of each feather and the body as indicated on the stencil. Carefully spread chocolate to the edges of the stencil outline using the back of a spoon. Melt dark chocolate, then spoon it onto the stencil to complete the feathers. Carefully spread dark chocolate within the stencil outline, joining it up to the milk chocolate. Place the baking sheet in the refrigerator until the chocolate is set.

Level the cake, turn it over, and place it on a serving plate.

Set a little ganache aside to use later, then cover the entire cake with ganache.

Once the chocolate turkey is completely set, remove it from the fridge, carefully peel away the parchment paper, and turn it upside down so that the flat surface is facing upward. Place the chocolate turkey on top of the cake.

TO MAKE THE EYES: Cut the marshmallow in half horizontally, turn the pieces cut side downward, then stick them in place on the turkey's face with a little ganache. Attach a chocolate chip to each marshmallow half with a dot of ganache.

TO MAKE THE BEAK: Cut 1 airplane-shaped candy into a beak shape, then stick it in place with a little ganache.

TO MAKE THE SNOOD: Cut the red fruit roll-up into 3-inch lengths. Cut each piece lengthwise and flatten it, then cut the ends to shape, as shown. Stick the snood in place with a little ganache.

TO MAKE THE FEET: Push one end of a toothpick into the tip of each of the remaining airplane-shaped candies. Insert the feet into the cake.

Bubbles

the colorful

FISH

TECHNIQUES

Coloring, page 24
Leveling, page 18
Crumb coating, page 18
Creating a smooth finish, page 18

WHAT YOU NEED

1 rectangular (9-by-13-inch) cake
  (see recipes, pages 12–13)
2 quantities buttercream (see recipe, page 20)
food colorings: blue & red
1 white chocolate disk
4 piping bags
4 extra-large round tips (Wilton 1A; optional)
1 large round tip (Wilton 6)
1 palette knife

STENCIL

Side D: Bubbles the Colorful Fish

INSTRUCTIONS

Bake the cake. Turn it out and leave it to cool completely.

Make the buttercream. Color half of it light blue. Divide the remaining half into 4 bowls and color the bowls of buttercream medium blue, blue, pink, and purple.

Level the cake and turn it over. Trace the fish stencil onto paper and cut it out. Place your stencil on the cake and cut out the body and the 2 fins. Place the cake pieces on a serving plate and stick on the fins with blue buttercream.

Crumb coat the cake with a thin layer of light blue buttercream. Refrigerate the cake until dry to the touch, then cover it with light blue buttercream to a smooth finish.

TO DECORATE THE FISH: Cut a 5½-inch-wide circle out of parchment paper and place it over the fish's face, as indicated on the stencil. Fit the extra-large round tips to the piping bags (or just cut off the tip of each piping bag to create an opening ½ inch in diameter) and fill 1 bag with medium blue, 1 with blue, 1 with pink, and 1 with purple buttercream. Starting at the base of the body, where it meets the tail, pipe large round dots of buttercream in a line, randomly alternating the 4 colors. Using a palette knife or the back of a teaspoon, press into the middle of each buttercream dot, smearing the dot toward the front of the fish to create the scale shapes. Repeat, piping the next line of dots in the joins between the scales of the first row, taking care to overlap the end of the previous smear. Continue the smeared brick-like pattern all the way up the body, smearing the last scales over the edge of the parchment paper covering the face. Carefully peel the parchment paper off, leaving a clean face shape with no scales.

TO MAKE THE EYE: Stick the white chocolate disk on with a little buttercream. Pipe the center of the eye with blue buttercream. Pipe big fat happy lips in the dark blue buttercream, as shown. Add a tiny spot of light blue buttercream to the eye so it appears to be catching the light.

Change the tip on the blue piping bag to the large round tip and pipe lines on the fins and tail, as shown.

my BUDDY

1 chocolate hemisphere cake (see recipe, page 13)

12 Oreo cookies

2 pink sugar wafers

2 red fruit roll-ups

2 quantities buttercream (see recipe, page 20)

Rice Krispies Treats (5 cups Rice Krispies & 2½ cups mini marshmallows; see recipe, page 14)

food colorings: black, red & yellow

2 tbsp cocoa powder

5 oz dark chocolate

1 giant purple gummy candy

2 black jelly beans

cooking spray, for molding Rice Krispies Treats

1 zippered plastic bag

1 skewer

1 piping bag

1 grass tip (Wilton 233)

1 rolling pin

1 bowl (3 by 6 inches approx.) and 5 small bowls (1½ by 3½ inches approx.)

TECHNIQUES

Melting chocolate, page 19
Coloring, page 24
Crumb coating, page 18
Cutting sugar wafers, page 19

STENCILS

Side C: My Buddy (ear, head, paw & snout)

INSTRUCTIONS

Bake the cake. Turn it out and leave it to cool completely.

TO MAKE THE EARS AND THE TAIL: Remove and discard the white center from each Oreo. Place all the Oreos into the zippered plastic bag and crush them with a rolling pin to a fine powder. Trace the dog ear stencil onto paper and cut it out. Place your stencil over one of the sugar wafers and cut out an ear shape using the tip of a sharp knife. Repeat with the second sugar wafer. To make the tail, roll one of the fruit roll-ups around a skewer, leaving the end of the log floppy. Melt dark chocolate, then dip each ear in the melted chocolate and then into the crushed Oreos so that the ears are completely covered. Repeat this process with the tail. Set the ears and tail aside on parchment paper to dry.

TO MAKE THE HEAD, SNOUT, AND PAWS: Trace the head, snout, and paw stencils onto paper and cut them out, then prepare 1 bowl and 5 small bowls by spraying them heavily with cooking oil. Make the Rice Krispies Treats. As soon as the mixture is cool enough to touch, spray cooking oil on your hands and press the mixture tightly into all 6 prepared bowls. The 4 paws need to be shallower than the snout, so fill 4 of the small bowls with less mixture than the fifth small bowl. You will need to work fast as the mixture will harden quickly.

Make the buttercream, color it light brown, adding cocoa to deepen the color if necessary. Once the cake is cool, put it back in the pan and use a serrated knife to cut any uneven rising off it to level it. Turn the cake out and crumb coat it with a thin layer of buttercream. Remove the Rice Krispies Treats shapes from their bowls, place your head, snout, and paws stencils on top of each shape, and use a sharp serrated knife to trim and round off the shapes if necessary. Cover the molded shapes in buttercream. Refrigerate the cake and shapes until dry to the touch.

Place the cake on a serving plate and arrange the Rice Krispies Treats head, snout and paw shapes into position around the cake. Fit the grass tip to the piping bag and fill the bag with buttercream. Pipe blobs of frosting while pulling up and away from the cake. Pipe clusters close together, ensuring the cake and Rice Krispies Treats surfaces are not showing through.

TO MAKE THE NOSE: Cut the giant gummy candy into a triangle. Use a little buttercream to stick the nose, ears, and jelly-bean eyes onto the dog's head.

TO MAKE THE COLLAR: Wrap the fruit roll-up around the dog's neck. Insert the skewer on the tail into the back of the cake.

2 rectangular (9-by-13-inch) cakes
   (see recipes, pages 12–13)
2 quantities buttercream (see recipe, page 20)
food colorings: red & yellow
2 oz white chocolate
26 oz dark chocolate
3 baking sheets
2 piping bags
1 offset spatula

TECHNIQUES

Coloring, page 24
Leveling, page 18
Crumb coating, page 18
Creating a smooth finish, page 18
Melting chocolate, page 19

STENCILS

Side D: The Mysterious Monarch
   (body & wing)

INSTRUCTIONS

Bake the cakes. Turn them out and leave them to cool completely.

Make the buttercream. Color 2 heaped tablespoons yellow and another 2 heaped tablespoons red. Color the remaining buttercream orange. Cover the bowls of buttercream with plastic wrap to prevent the frosting from drying out.

Level the cakes and turn them over. Trace only the outline of the butterfly wing stencil onto paper and cut it out. Place the wing stencil on 1 cake and cut 1 wing shape out of cake. Turn the wing stencil over (so you have a left and a right wing), place it on the second cake and cut out the second wing. Arrange the 2 cake wings on a serving plate, joining them together with a little orange buttercream to form a butterfly shape.

Crumb coat the cake with a thin layer of orange buttercream, then refrigerate it until dry to the touch. Cover the cake with buttercream to a smooth finish. Add a little red and a little yellow buttercream to the middle of the cake where the wings meet (red toward the top and yellow toward the bottom, as shown) and use an offset spatula to smoothly blend the colors into the orange buttercream.

TO MAKE THE WING MARKINGS: Trace the wing stencil, including all the butterfly's markings, onto a large piece of parchment paper. Repeat on another piece of parchment paper for the second wing. Lay each wing stencil on separate baking sheets, turning one over so that you have a left wing and a right wing. Stick the stencils to the baking sheets with a little buttercream.

Melt the white chocolate. Once the chocolate has cooled slightly, pour it into a piping bag, then cut a tiny portion off the tip of the bag. Pipe white chocolate into the small spots on the wings.

Melt the dark chocolate. Once the dark chocolate has cooled slightly, fill another piping bag. Cut off the tip of the piping bag, then thickly pipe on the dark markings, covering the white chocolate spots as you go. When dry to the touch, apply a second layer of dark chocolate over the first for added strength.

Put the sheets of wings in the fridge to set. Trace the butterfly body stencil onto a piece of parchment paper, cut it out, and lay it on another baking sheet. Thickly pipe dark chocolate over the body shape, then place the sheet in the fridge to set.

Once the wing markings and body are completely set, remove them from the fridge and carefully peel the parchment paper away. Gently turn over each wing so that the white spotty side faces upward, then arrange the wings on the cake so that they meet in the middle. Finally, turn the body piece over and arrange it over the wings, securing it in place with a small amount of buttercream on its underside.

INSTRUCTIONS

Bake the cake. Turn it out and leave it to cool completely.

Make the fondant pigs, using the picture as your guide.

TO MAKE THE PIGS THAT ARE FLOATING ON THEIR BACKS: First make their tummies by shaping ¾ oz pink fondant into a ball and cutting the ball in half. Using a skewer, poke a belly button into the middle of each tummy. To make the heads, shape ¼ oz pink fondant into a smaller ball and cut this in half. Use more pink fondant to make 2 small, flat circular noses. Attach the noses to the top of each of the smaller half circles with a little water. Use the skewer to poke 2 nostrils in each nose and 2 eyeholes above the nose. For the ears, attach 2 small triangles to the side of each head, near the top, with a little water. Make 8 small ¼-inch long cylinders and turn these into feet by pressing a V shape in the end of each with the skewer. Keep the tummy, head, and feet separate, as you will arrange them later when you put them on the cake.

TO MAKE THE DIVING PIG: Shape ¾ oz pink fondant into a ball and cut it in half. Discard one half. Roll a skinny length of pink fondant and twist it around the end of the skewer to make a spring shape. Stick the twisty spring-shaped tail to the top of the half ball with a spot of water. Make 2 more feet as described above.

TO MAKE THE SITTING PIGS: Start by making the first sitting pig's tummy. Roll ¾ oz of pink fondant into a ball and use the skewer to poke a belly button into the middle of it. For the head, roll another ball out of ¼ oz of pink fondant and attach it to the top of the tummy like you're making a snowman. Make a small, flat circular nose and attach it to the front of the head with a spot of water. Use the skewer to poke 2 nostrils in the nose and 2 eyeholes above the nose. For the ears, attach 1 triangle on either side of the head with a spot of water. Make 2 more feet as described above. Stick these to either side of the body, below the head, with a spot of water. Repeat this process to make the second pig.

TO MAKE THE PARTY HATS: Shape a small amount of white fondant into a ¾-inch-high cone with a small ball the size of a pinhead on top. Roll a long, skinny length of pink fondant and wrap it around the cone on the diagonal, sticking it on with a little water. Repeat this process for the other 3 hats, then stick the hats to the pigs' heads with a little water. For the present, make a small box out of the leftover white fondant. Roll a long, skinny length of pink fondant and wrap it around the box like a ribbon, as shown, sticking it on with a little water.

Make the ganache. Level the cake. When the ganache has started to cool and has a consistency similar to corn syrup, place the cake on a wire rack and pour the ganache over the cake, letting the excess run off.

Press chocolate pirouettes into the ganache around the edge of the cake, making sure that they stick up slightly over the lip of the cake. Gently wrap string around the cake to hold the pirouettes in place until the ganache sets. Arrange the pigs on top of the cake and gently press them into the ganache.

Once the ganache is set, carefully place the cake on a serving plate and remove the string.

Note
The pigs can be made up to a week in advance.

INSTRUCTIONS

Bake the cakes. Turn them out and leave them to cool completely.

Trace the stencils onto parchment paper and cut them out. Thinly roll out assorted fondant for making the animals to a thickness of ⅛ inch and cut out the shapes, using your stencils as a guide as well as the mini shapes and daisy-shaped-cutters, as follows:

Giraffe
Yellow: 1 large oval, 1 rectangle & 2 small hearts
Brown: 1 small heart cut into halves, 1 small circle & 4 spots

Elephant
Light blue: 1 elephant stencil & 2 large hearts

Hippo
Purple: 1 large circle & 2 small hearts
Light purple: 1 large oval

Monkey
Brown: 1 medium circle & 2 extra-small circles
Light brown: 1 small oval & 2 spots

Lion
Orange: 1 large daisy flower
Yellow: 1 large circle & 2 small hearts
White: 2 spots
Pink: 1 teardrop
Black: 1 extra-small triangle

Zebra
White: 1 large oval & 2 small hearts
Black: 1 small oval & 5 small triangles

Using the picture as a guide, stick each animal together, using a little water as glue between each layer. Use the black edible-ink pen or a toothpick dipped in black gel food coloring to draw on eyes and the monkey's round nose.

Use the skewer to push nostrils into the giraffe, hippo, and zebra's faces. Draw smiles on the giraffe and monkey and make dots on the lion's snout.

Set the animal faces aside to dry on parchment paper.

The ANIMAL Circus

WHAT YOU NEED

1 chocolate princess cake (see recipe, page 13)

1 round (8-inch) cake (see recipes, pages 12–13)

fondant, for animals: 1 oz each yellow, brown, light brown, light blue, purple, light purple, orange, pink, white & black

fondant, for cake: 1 lb red, 2 lb white, 4½ oz black & 5 oz blue

1 quantity buttercream or ganache (see recipes, pages 20–21)

1 black edible-ink pen or black gel food coloring

cornstarch, for rolling out fondant

toothpicks

mini shape cutters (see page 17)

daisy-shaped cutter (see page 17)

1 skewer

1 rolling pin

STENCILS

Side D: The Animal Circus (circles, elephant, hearts & ovals)

TECHNIQUES

Rolling out fondant, page 21
Leveling, page 18
Stacking & filling, page 18
Creating a smooth finish, page 18
Covering a cake with fondant, page 23

The Animal Circus continues on page 80 . . .

The ANIMAL Circus

CONTINUED

TO MAKE THE FLAG: Thinly roll out a small portion of red fondant to a thickness of ⅛ inch and cut out a 1¼ inch long triangle for the flag. Wrap the wide end of the flag around the end of a toothpick. Lay the flag over another 2 toothpicks to create bumps, giving the flag a windblown effect. Set the flag aside to dry.

Make the buttercream or ganache.

Level the round cake. Place the princess cake back in the pan and use a serrated knife to cut any uneven rising off the cake to level it. Turn the princess cake out, place it on top of the round cake and trim the edges to match. Remove the princess cake, cover the top of the round cake with buttercream or ganache, then stack the princess cake back on top.

Place the stacked cake on a serving plate and cover it with buttercream or ganache to a smooth finish. Roll out 30 oz white fondant to a thickness of ¼ inch and a diameter of about 18 inches. Place fondant over the cake, then smooth and trim it.

TO MAKE THE RED STRIPES FOR THE TENT: Roll out red fondant to a thickness of ¼ inch, then cut out 16 strips each measuring 8½ inches long and ¾ inch wide at one end, tapering to ½ inch wide at the other end. Stick the red stripes to the cake with a little water, positioning the tapered ends at the top of the cake and leaving a ¾ inch gap between each stripe at the base.

TO MAKE THE OPENING FOR THE TENT: Roll out black fondant to a thickness of ¼ inch, then cut out a 6-inch-high triangle with a 5-inch-wide base. Stick the black triangle to the front of the cake, overlapping the stripes, with a little water. Roll out white fondant to a thickness of ¼ inch and cut out 2 triangles that are 6 inches high with a 1¼-inch-wide base. Use a little water to stick a white triangle to each side of the black triangle to create tent flaps.

TO MAKE THE BUNTING: Thinly roll out blue fondant to a thickness of ⅛ inch, then cut out 40 triangles using a small triangle cutter. Use a small amount of water to stick approximately 24 blue triangles in a line around the cake, starting just above the tent flap. From the white fondant cut out a white circle with a 3-inch diameter and place it on top of the cake. Stick the remaining triangles around the edge of the white circle with a little water. Form a small cone the size and shape of a thimble from white fondant. Place it on top of the white circle and insert the flag into the middle of the cone.

Stick the animal faces to the black fondant, as shown, using a small amount of buttercream or ganache.

STEGGY
the friendly
DINOSAUR

TECHNIQUES

Coloring, page 24
Leveling, page 18
Crumb coating, page 18
Creating a smooth finish, page 18

STENCILS

Side B: Steggy the Friendly Dinosaur (back leg, body, front leg, head & tail)

WHAT YOU NEED

1 round (8-inch) cake (see recipes, pages 12–13)
1 round (10-inch) cake (see recipes, pages 12–13)
1 quantity buttercream (see recipe, page 20)
food coloring: green
2 Mallomars
10 large white chocolate disks
30 (approx.) small milk chocolate disks
2 Whoppers malted milk balls
1 x 14-oz Toblerone bar

INSTRUCTIONS

Bake the cakes. Turn the cakes out and leave them to cool completely.

Make the buttercream and color it light green.

Trace the stencils onto paper and cut them out. Level the cakes and turn them over. Place your stencils on the cakes and cut out the shapes. Cut the head and the tail out of the 8-inch cake, and the body and the legs out of the 10-inch cake.

Stand the body on its straight edge on your serving plate and stick the legs, head, and tail in place, as shown on the next page, with buttercream. Crumb coat the cake with a thin layer of buttercream. Refrigerate until dry to the touch.

Cover the cake with buttercream to a smooth finish.

TO MAKE THE EYES: Place 2 Mallomars on the head, as shown. Stick a white chocolate disk and then a smaller milk chocolate disk to the front of each Mallomars with a little buttercream.

TO MAKE THE NOSTRILS: Press 2 Whoppers into the buttercream in front of the eyes.

TO MAKE THE TEETH: Cut the remaining white chocolate disks into quarters and stick them into the front of the head with the points facing down.

FOR THE TOES: Place 3 milk chocolate disks at the end of each foot for toes. Randomly press the rest of the milk chocolate disks into the buttercream all over the dinosaur's body.

TO MAKE THE DINOSAUR'S SPIKES: Break the Toblerone bar into individual pieces. Press 1 piece into the top of the dinosaur's body, then cut the next 2 pieces ¼ inch shorter and press them into the buttercream on either side of the first spike. Repeat this process along the back and down the tail of the dinosaur, cutting each Toblerone spike ¼ inch shorter than the last spike.

⊰RUBBER DUCKY⊱

2 rectangular (9-by-13-inch) cakes (see recipes, pages 12–13)

Rice Krispies Treats (9 cups Rice Krispies
& 4½ cups mini marshmallows; see recipe, page 14)

2 quantities buttercream (see recipe, page 20)

food colorings: blue & yellow

3½ cups shredded coconut

2 orange airplane-shaped gummy candies

2 oz white chocolate

1 licorice stick

2 large, flat round white mints,
or other similar candy

1 giant licorice allsort

1 package round white candies

cooking spray, for molding Rice Krispies Treats

1 skewer

1 zippered plastic bag

4 toothpicks

1 piping bag

STENCIL

Side C: Rubber Ducky (wing)

TECHNIQUES

Coloring, page 24; Leveling, page 18; Crumb coating, page 18; Creating a smooth finish, page 18; Stacking & filling, page 18; Coloring coconut, page 19; Melting chocolate, page 19; Cutting sugar wafers, page 19

INSTRUCTIONS

Bake the cakes. Turn them out and leave them to cool completely.

TO MAKE THE HEAD: Make the Rice Krispies Treats using 5 cups of the Rice Krispies and 3½ cups of the marshmallows. As soon as the mixture is cool enough to touch, spray cooking oil on your hands and mold the mixture into a rounded ball shape. Set the head aside to cool and harden.

TO MAKE THE WINGS: Trace 2 duck wing stencils onto parchment paper. Turn 1 of your wing stencils over so you have both left and right wings. Repeat the Rice Krispies Treats recipe, using the remaining 4 cups Rice Krispies and 2½ cups marshmallows. As soon as the mixture is cool enough to touch, shape it into 2 duck wings, pressing it onto the parchment paper stencils to create the wing shapes. Set the wings aside to cool and harden. Once hard, peel away the parchment paper and use a sharp serrated knife to shape the Rice Krispies Treats wings if necessary.

Make the buttercream, divide it evenly into 2 bowls and color one bowl yellow and the other bowl blue. Level the cakes. Crumb coat 1 rectangular cake with a thin layer of blue buttercream. Refrigerate the cake until dry to the touch, then place it on your serving plate. Cover the cake with blue buttercream to a smooth finish.

TO MAKE THE BODY: Cut the other rectangular cake into 3 equal widths and stack and fill it with yellow buttercream. Using a serrated knife, carve the corners off the cake stack to make a long oval. Carve a curved slope along the top of the body, finishing with a tip to form the tail, as shown. Round off

the body so there are no sharp edges except for the pointy tail at the back. Stick a skewer into the Rice Krispies Treats head and insert it into the front of the body. Stick a toothpick into each Rice Krispies Treats wing and insert the wings into each side of the body, securing them with buttercream.

Color the coconut yellow. Cover the entire duck with yellow buttercream. Sit the duck in a roasting pan or similar to catch the mess, then press the yellow coconut into the buttercream until the duck is completely covered. Brush off any excess coconut, then place the duck cake on the middle of the blue rectangular cake.

TO MAKE THE BEAK: Cut the wide end of both the airplane-shaped gummy candies into a curve so they will sit flush against the duck's head. Insert a toothpick into the cut curve of each plane and then push the shaped plane into the front of the duck's head, angling them to make an open beak.

Melt the white chocolate, spoon it into a piping bag, and cut a tiny tip off the pointy end of the bag. To make the eyes, cut 2 thin slices off the licorice stick and glue one to each of the large, flat mints using the white chocolate. Pipe a dot of white chocolate on each pupil, as shown. Stick the eyes to the duck's head with the melted chocolate.

TO MAKE THE EYELASHES: Separate the layers of the giant allsort, then cut the licorice layers into comb shapes. Use the melted chocolate to glue the eyelashes above each eye.

FOR THE BUBBLES: Arrange the round white candies around the duck's body on the blue cake, sticking them on with white chocolate if necessary.

fondant: 2½ lb white, 9 oz navy blue, 1 oz red, 9 oz pale
    ice blue, ½ lb light blue, 7 oz medium blue & 6 oz blue
Rice Krispies Treats (3 cups Rice Krispies & 1½ cups mini
    marshmallows; see recipe, page 14)
1 quantity buttercream or ganache (see recipes, pages 20–21)
1¾ oz white chocolate
2 round (8-inch) cakes (see recipes, pages 12–13)
cornstarch, for rolling out fondant
cooking spray, for molding Rice Krispies Treats
1 black edible-ink pen (optional)
1 skewer
2 toothpicks
1 small rolling pin

STENCILS

Side D: "Flying Cloud" (boat & sails)

TECHNIQUES

Rolling out fondant, page 21
Melting chocolate, page 19
Leveling, page 18
Stacking & filling, page 18
Creating a smooth finish, page 18
Covering a cake with fondant, page 23
Coloring, page 24

INSTRUCTIONS

Make the sails and flag at least a day in advance to allow for drying time.

TO MAKE THE SAILS AND FLAG: Trace the sails stencil onto paper and cut it out. Thinly roll out 3½ oz white fondant to a thickness of ⅛ inch, place the sails stencil on the fondant and cut out the sails shape. Thinly roll out 2¾ oz of navy blue fondant and cut it into ½-inch-wide strips long enough to make stripes on one side of the sails. Using a little water, stick alternating navy blue stripes onto the sails, as shown. Thinly roll out a very small portion of red fondant and cut out a small triangle for the flag. Lay the flag over 2 toothpicks to make bumps in the flag, creating a windblown effect. Set the sails and flag aside in a warm dry space to harden overnight.

TO MAKE THE BOAT: Trace the boat stencil onto parchment paper and cut it out. Make the Rice Krispies Treats. As soon as the mixture is cool enough to touch, spray cooking oil on your hands and mold and compress the mixture with your hands into a general boat shape. (Don't be too concerned if it is not perfect, as you will be able to trim and shape the boat with a serrated knife once it is set.) Work quickly, as the Rice Krispies

Treats only take a couple of minutes to harden. Once hard, place the Rice Krispies Treats boat over your stencil and use a serrated knife to shape it.

Make the buttercream or ganache. Cover the boat in buttercream or ganache, filling all the holes so the boat is smooth. Roll out 5 oz white fondant to a thickness of ¼ inch and use this to cover the boat, smoothing out the fondant and tucking the edges underneath. Thinly roll out a small portion of red fondant, cut a ½-inch-wide strip and stick this around the base of the boat with a little water. At this point, you can write a name, like Flying Cloud, on the side of your boat with a black edible-ink pen if you desire.

Once the sail has hardened, melt white chocolate. Lay the hardened sail striped side down. Spoon a thin line of melted chocolate down the middle of the sail and stick on the skewer to make a mast, leaving ½ inch of the skewer sticking up above the sail to attach the flag to later. Once the chocolate has cooled and hardened around the skewer, dip the top of the skewer in melted white chocolate and stick the flag to the top.

"Flying Cloud" continues on page 88 . . .

"*Flying Cloud*"

CONTINUED

Bake the cakes. Turn them out and leave them to cool completely. Level the cakes, then stack and fill them with buttercream or ganache. Place the cake on a serving plate and cover it in buttercream or ganache to a smooth finish. Roll out 1¾ lb white fondant to ¼ inch thick and a diameter of 16 inches. Place the fondant on the cake, then smooth and trim it.

TO MAKE THE WAVES: Thinly roll out the pale ice blue fondant to a thickness of ⅛ inch. Cut out a rectangular strip 4 inches wide by 24 inches long. Cut a shallow wave pattern along the top of the strip, allowing a ¾–1¼-inch difference between the peaks and the troughs. Try to begin and end with the peak or trough of a wave so the strip will join seamlessly at the back of the cake. Brush a little water around the side of the cake so that the wave will stick to it. Carefully roll the pale ice blue fondant up around a small rolling pin dusted with cornstarch, so that you can lift it to the cake without tearing or stretching its shape. Holding the rolling pin vertically, unroll the fondant around the cake, gently sticking it to the damp fondant underneath as you go. Trim any excess length where the fondant meets at the back of the cake, then secure both ends with a little water.

Repeat the wave-making process with the light blue fondant, rolling out a rectangle 4 inches wide. Brush the outside of the pale ice blue waves on the cake with a little water then, using the same technique, stick the second line of waves to the cake, making sure the peaks and troughs of the 2 sets of waves don't line up. Repeat with the remaining blue fondants, rolling out rectangles to a width of 3 inches for the medium blue fondant, 2½ inches for the blue, and 2 inches for the navy blue. Use a finger to gently pull the peak of each wave out from the side of the cake to give the waves a 3-D look.

Carefully place the boat on the middle of the cake, then push the skewer, with the sails attached, through the center of the boat and down into the cake for support.

CHUBBY penguin ISLAND

1 round (10-inch) cake (see recipes, pages 12–13)
2 quantities royal icing (see recipe, page 20)
2 ice cream sugar cones (see page 19)
1½ cups shredded coconut
fondant: 1 oz black, ⅓ oz white & ¾ oz orange
1 quantity buttercream with vegetable
  shortening base (see recipe, page 20)

food colorings: black & blue
Rice Krispies Treats (5 cups Rice
  Krispies & 2½ cups mini
  marshmallows; see recipe, page 14)
cornstarch, for rolling out fondant
cooking spray, for molding
  Rice Krispies Treats

1 piping bag
1 skewer
1 palette knife
1 rolling pin

TECHNIQUES

Rolling out fondant, page 21
Coloring, page 24
Leveling, page 18
Crumb coating, page 18
Creating a smooth finish, page 18

INSTRUCTIONS

Make the igloo base, coconut trees, and penguins at least a day in advance of serving.

Bake the cake. Turn it out and leave it to cool completely.

Prepare the royal icing. Add 1 tablespoon to a piping bag and set the bag aside for later.

TO MAKE THE ICY SHARDS ON THE IGLOO: Line a baking sheet with parchment paper and thinly spread the surface of the entire tray with 1/16 inch of royal icing using a palette knife. Place the tray in a cool oven on the lowest heat for approximately 1 hour or until the icing has dried. (The parchment paper will crinkle up, creating texture on one side of the shards.)

TO MAKE THE TREES: Cut 1¼–2 inches off the wide end of 1 sugar ice cream cone. Spread royal icing over both cones, then roll the cones in shredded coconut until both are well covered. Stand the cones facing down on a piece of parchment paper and leave them to dry.

TO MAKE THE PENGUINS: Divide black fondant into 3 equal parts (approximately ⅓ oz each) and roll them into ovals. Thinly roll out white fondant to a thickness of ⅛ inch and cut out 3 circles approximately ½ inch in diameter. (An easy way to do this is to use the open end of a piping tip as a punch.) Stick a white "tummy" circle to the front of each oval using a dot of the reserved royal icing. Roll 6 orange fondant balls, each the size of a pinhead. Flatten the orange balls to make feet and stick 2 below the white circle on each penguin using a dot of royal icing. Roll another 6 pinhead-sized orange fondant balls and form them into triangles. Make a beak shape by attaching 2 orange triangles to each face. Cut a tiny tip off the bag of white royal icing, which you set aside earlier, and pipe 2 white eyes on each penguin. Once the eyes are dry, use the tip of a skewer dipped in black food coloring to draw a black dot in the middle of each white eye.

Make the buttercream with a vegetable shortening base and color it pale ice blue.

Chubby Penguin Island continues on page 90 . . .

CHUBBY
penguin
ISLAND

CONTINUED

Level the cake, crumb coat it with a thin layer of buttercream, then refrigerate it until dry to the touch.

Place the cake on a serving plate, then cover the cake with buttercream to a smooth finish. Pour the remaining royal icing on the center of the cake and carefully spread it out until it just dribbles over the edge of the cake. Allow the royal icing to set.

TO MAKE THE IGLOO: Prepare a cereal bowl (3 by 6 inches approximately) and a small flat-bottomed ramekin (2 by 3½ inches approximately) by spraying them heavily with cooking oil. Make the Rice Krispies Treats. As soon as the mixture is cool enough to touch, spray cooking oil on your hands and press the mixture tightly into the prepared bowl and ramekin. Set the molds aside for approximately 10 minutes until the Rice Krispies Treats have cooled and hardened, then pop out the shapes. Cut off one-third of the small ramekin circle with a serrated knife, then use the larger portion to create the igloo's doorway. Stand the doorway up on its flat edge and stick it to the cereal bowl dome with a small amount of buttercream to form the igloo. Cover the igloo with buttercream and place it on the cake. Break the shards of dried royal icing into irregular pieces and press them, textured side up, into the fresh buttercream on the igloo, leaving an opening in the front for the doorway.

Arrange the coconut trees and penguins around the igloo.

Notes
The igloo and trees will keep well in airtight containers for a couple of days, and the penguins will keep in a separate airtight container for 2 months.

When dribbling the white icing over the edge of the cake, go slowly to ensure the icing doesn't run off the bottom of the cake.

INSTRUCTIONS

Make the ganache and set it aside to firm up.

Bake the cakes. Turn them out and leave them to cool completely.

Level the round cake. Place the princess cake back in the pan and use a serrated knife to cut any uneven rising off the cake to level it. Turn the cake out. Place the princess cake on top of the round cake and trim the edges to match. Remove the princess cake, cover the top of round cake with ganache, then place the princess cake back on top.

TO MAKE THE CRATER: Use a sharp knife and a teaspoon to carve out a 1¼-inch-wide round hole in the top of the cake. Crumb coat the cake with a thin layer of ganache, then refrigerate the cake until dry to the touch.

Cover the cake with ganache to a smooth finish. Set aside a small amount of ganache for sticking the trees onto the cake later.

TO MAKE THE LAVA: Make royal icing to flood consistency. Evenly divide the royal icing among 3 bowls and color 1 red, 1 orange, and 1 yellow. Cover the bowls with plastic wrap to prevent the icing from drying out. Place the cake on a wire rack and lay a sheet of aluminum foil or parchment paper underneath it to catch any run-off mess. Spoon the royal icing lava onto the top of the cake, letting it run down the sides. Alternate colors to create a fiery lava effect.

TO MAKE THE PALM TREES: Cut 8 chocolate-covered gummy sticks in half lengthwise. Press halves end to end, directly onto the cake to create palm tree trunks, sticking them on with a small amount of ganache if necessary. Use extra ganache to stick 4–5 spearmint leaves to the top of each tree trunk to make fronds.

Once the ganache is completely dry and the palm trees are stuck to the cake, carefully lift the cake onto a serving plate, using a large offset spatula.

Add sparklers to the crater of the volcano (or candles if sparklers are unavailable).

THE Fiery MOUNTAIN

WHAT YOU NEED

1 quantity milk chocolate ganache (see recipe, page 21)
1 chocolate princess cake (see recipe, page 13)
1 round (8-inch) cake (see recipes, pages 12–13)
1 quantity royal icing (see recipe, page 20)
food colorings: red & yellow
8 chocolate-covered gummy sticks
35 (approx.) spearmint leaves candy
4–6 sparklers or candles
1 large offset spatula

TECHNIQUES

Leveling, page 18
Crumb coating, page 18
Creating a smooth finish, page 18
Royal icing (flood consistency), page 20
Coloring, page 24

Treasure
ISLAND

WHAT YOU NEED

2 round (8-inch) cakes (see recipes, pages 12–13)

Rice Krispies Treats (3½ cups Rice Krispies & 1¾ cups mini marshmallows; see recipe, page 14)

3½ oz dark or milk chocolate

6 x 1½-oz packages Kit Kat bars (24 wafers)

2 quantities buttercream (see recipe, page 20)

food colorings: black, blue, red & yellow

3½ oz vanilla wafer cookies

1 package chocolate gold coins

1 packet small round mints

1 packet lollipops

cooking spray, for molding Rice Krispies Treats

2 piping bags

1 large open star tip (Wilton 199)

2 zippered plastic bags

1 rolling pin

1 palette knife

TECHNIQUES

Melting chocolate, page 19

Coloring, page 24

Leveling, page 18

Crumb coating, page 18

Stacking & filling, page 18

Creating a smooth finish, page 18

Piping techniques (waves), page 29

INSTRUCTIONS

Bake the cakes. Turn them out and leave them to cool completely.

TO MAKE THE TREASURE CHEST: Make Rice Krispies Treats. As soon as the mixture is cool enough to touch, spray cooking oil on your hands, then mold and compress the mixture into a rectangular box shape, approximately 3 by 3½ by 2½ inches. Work quickly, as the Rice Krispies Treats only take a couple of minutes to harden. Once your molded shape is hard, use a serrated knife to shape it into a 3-by-3½-by-2½-inch box.

Melt 2 oz of the chocolate, spoon it into a piping bag, then cut a tiny portion off the tip of the bag. Unwrap 4 Kit Kat bars (16 wafers) and, using the melted chocolate as glue, stick the bars to the sides of the Rice Krispies Treats rectangle.

TO MAKE THE TREASURE CHEST LID: Unwrap the remaining 2 Kit Kat bars (8 wafers). Carefully break 1 wafer off 1 of the bars, leaving a 3-wafer bar. Use the melted chocolate to stick the 3-wafer bar and the other full, 4-wafer bar together, then set the 7-wafer lid aside to dry on parchment paper.

Make the buttercream. Set two-thirds aside and color the remaining third light brown.

Level the cakes, then stack and fill them with light brown buttercream. Place the cake on a serving plate.

TO MAKE THE SAND: Place cookies in a zippered plastic bag and use a rolling pin to crush them into a sandy texture. Cover the top of the cake and ¾ inch down the side with brown buttercream to a smooth finish. Sprinkle sand over the cake, pressing it into the buttercream down the sides of the cake to make it stick.

TO PIPE THE WAVES: Color the reserved two-thirds of the buttercream turquoise. Using a palette knife, lightly coat the sides of the cake, below the sand, in turquoise buttercream (so any gaps in the piped waves will be less noticeable). Fit the large open star tip to the piping bag and half fill it with turquoise buttercream. Starting at the top of the cake, just slightly overlapping the bottom edge of the sand, pipe a row of turquoise waves. Squeeze any leftover buttercream in the piping bag back into the turquoise buttercream bowl, add a few more drops of blue food coloring to make a darker shade, and refill the piping bag. Pipe a row of darker waves under the first. Continue piping waves down the side of the cake, adding more blue coloring to the buttercream for each row to create an ombré wave effect.

Place the treasure chest on the middle of the cake and sprinkle some of the crushed cookies around its base to make it look like it is slightly buried in the sand. Melt the rest of the chocolate and use it to stick chocolate gold coins in the top of the treasure chest. Use melted chocolate to stick the lid (propped open by the chocolate gold coins) on the treasure chest.

TO MAKE THE STRING OF PEARLS: Use melted chocolate to stick on a line of small mints that appear to be spilling out of the open treasure chest.

TO MAKE THE JEWELS: Put lollipops in a zippered plastic bag, cover the bag with a kitchen towel and bang the bag with a rolling pin to break lollipops into chunks. Discard the sticks. Sprinkle the lollipop jewels around the gold coins in the treasure chest and in the sand around the base of the treasure chest.

The "ARR-ME-HEARTIES!" CUPCAKES

WHAT YOU NEED

12 cupcakes (see recipes, pages 12–13)
1 quantity royal icing (see recipe, page 20)
gel food colorings: black, red & yellow
lollipops (optional)
chocolate gold coins (optional)
3 piping bags
3 small round tips (Wilton 3) or use 1 tip and wash it between colors
toothpicks
12 gold foil cupcake liners
1 zippered plastic bag (optional)
1 rolling pin (optional)

INSTRUCTIONS

Bake the cupcakes in the gold foil cupcake liners and leave them to cool completely.

Make the royal icing. Fit a small round tip to a piping bag, add 1 tablespoon of uncolored icing to the bag, then set it aside. Place another heaped tablespoon of icing in a small bowl and color it black. Separate the remaining royal icing, placing one-third in one bowl and coloring it red and two-thirds in another bowl and coloring it your color of choice for faces (peach shown). Cover the bowls with plastic wrap to prevent the icing from drying out, then set them aside.

TO MAKE THE PIRATE FACES: Level the cupcakes. Fit a round tip to a new piping bag and place a heaped tablespoon of peach royal icing into the bag. Pipe a circle outline around the edge of all the cupcakes. Slowly add drops of water to the bowl of peach royal icing until it reaches flood consistency. Spoon the flood consistency royal icing into the middle of each cupcake and use a toothpick to evenly spread the icing to the outline. Put the cupcakes aside until the peach icing is dry. Keep the bag of peach icing for using later.

TO MAKE THE RED BANDANNAS: Once the peach icing is dry to the touch (be gentle, as it will still be wet below the surface), fit a small round tip to a new piping bag and place a heaped tablespoon of red royal icing inside the bag. Pipe an outline of a semicircle, with the flat edge slightly above the centerline of the cupcake, to make the pirate's bandanna.

Slowly add drops of water to the bowl of red royal icing until it reaches flood consistency. Spoon the flood consistency red royal icing inside the bandanna outline, using a toothpick to spread it evenly. While the red icing is still wet, take the bag of uncolored royal icing and pipe white spots randomly all over the red outline (the spots will sink into the wet red icing and dry flat).

Use the peach royal icing to pipe a small round nose on each cupcake. Use the white royal icing to pipe a small eye. Once the white eye is dry to the touch, dip a toothpick in the black royal icing and use it to dot a black pupil on the eye and to draw a small mouth.

When the red bandanna icing is dry to the touch, dip a toothpick in black royal icing and use it to draw an eye patch on each cupcake.

For optional decoration, put lollipops inside a zippered plastic bag, cover the bag with a kitchen towel, then bang the bag with a rolling pin to break the lollipops into chunks. Discard the sticks. Sprinkle the lollipop jewels, along with chocolate gold coins, around the cupcakes.

2 round (8-inch) cakes (see recipes, pages 12–13)

fondant: 1¾ oz yellow, ⅓ oz navy blue & 2½ oz color of choice for skin (peach shown)

1 quantity buttercream (see recipe, page 20)

½ quantity royal icing (see recipe, page 20)

gel food colorings: black, blue & red

cornstarch, for rolling out fondant

4 piping bags

2 small star tips (Wilton 30)

1 small round tip (Wilton 3)

toothpicks

1 rolling pin

STENCILS

Side D: Dive In (arm, head & flipper)

TECHNIQUES

Rolling out fondant, page 21

Coloring, page 24

Leveling, page 18

Crumb coating, page 18

Stacking & filling, page 18

Creating a smooth finish, page 18

INSTRUCTIONS

Bake the cakes. Turn them out and leave them to cool completely.

Trace the arm, flipper, and head stencils onto parchment paper, then cut them out.

TO MAKE THE SNORKEL: Using your hands, roll a small rope of yellow fondant measuring ⅛ inch wide and 2 inches long. Bend it into a J shape and leave it to dry.

TO MAKE THE FLIPPERS: Divide the remaining yellow fondant into 2 equal portions and mold each into a flipper using the stencil as a guide. Using a finger, press 3 indents into the top edge of each flipper, as shown. Thinly roll out navy blue fondant to a thickness of ⅛ inch. Cut 2 strips wide enough to wrap around the bottom half of each flipper. Stick the blue strips onto the flippers with a little water and trim off the excess blue fondant where it meets at the back of each flipper. Insert a toothpick halfway into the bottom of each flipper and set the flippers aside.

Make the buttercream, color it blue, and set 2 tablespoons aside.

Make the royal icing. Put 2 heaped tablespoons in a bowl and color it black. Fit a small star tip to a piping bag and fill the bag with black icing. Put 2 heaped tablespoons of royal icing in another bowl and color it red. Fit a small round tip to a piping bag and fill it with red icing. Put 2 heaped tablespoons of uncolored royal icing in a piping bag and cut a tiny portion off the tip of the bag.

Level the cakes, then stack and fill them with buttercream. Crumb coat the cake with a thin layer of buttercream, then refrigerate it until dry to the touch. Place the cake on a serving plate and cover the cake with buttercream to a smooth finish.

TO MAKE THE FACE AND HAIR: Thinly roll out peach fondant to a thickness of ⅛ inch. Place the head and arm stencils on the fondant and cut out the shapes. Press the shapes into the buttercream on the front of the cake (use a little royal icing to stick them on if the buttercream is too dry). Pipe black hair on top of the fondant head. Remember that underwater hair floats in all directions, so have fun with it! Use the white royal icing to pipe 2 eyes on the face. Use the red royal icing to pipe a mask around the eyes. Dip a toothpick in blue buttercream and make a small blue dot in the center of each eye. Dip a toothpick in the black food coloring and carefully make a dot in the center of each blue dot.

Mix a small amount of leftover red and white royal icing in a small bowl to make pink. Dip a toothpick in the pink royal icing and use it to make a small round mouth. Stick the yellow J-shaped snorkel in place with white royal icing. Use the white royal icing to pipe mini waves around the swimmer's hands and bubbles out of the top of the snorkel.

Fit a small star tip to a piping bag and fill it with 2 heaped tablespoons of leftover buttercream. Insert the flippers into the top of the cake and pipe water splashes around them with blue buttercream.

½ quantity dark chocolate ganache
 (see recipe, page 21)
10 cupcakes (see recipes, pages 12–13)
1 quantity buttercream (see recipe, page 20)
food colorings: green, red & yellow

½ cup dark chocolate chips
15 (approx.) gumdrops
1 tbsp honey
3 sugar ice cream cones
1 tbsp multicolor sprinkles
1 Cadbury Flake bar

10 cupcake liners
1 piping bag
1 skewer
1 palette knife

TECHNIQUE

Coloring, page 24

THE
icy, creamy
CUPCAKES

INSTRUCTIONS

Make the ganache and set it aside to firm up.

Bake the cupcakes in liners and leave them to cool completely.

Put 2 tablespoons of ganache into a piping bag and set aside. Whip the rest of the ganache with an electric mixer until fluffy and lighter in color.

Make the buttercream and divide it equally among 4 bowls. Leave 2 bowls uncolored, then color 1 bowl orange and the other bowl mint green. When you are ready to frost the red-swirl cupcakes, add a few drops of red food coloring to one bowl of plain buttercream, stirring only once to create a swirled effect.

TO MAKE THE SCOOPS OF ICE CREAM: Using a palette knife, frost each cupcake roughly in a circular motion so that it looks like a scoop of ice cream. Use each of the colored buttercreams and the whipped ganache, frosting the cupcakes with different colors. For the orange cupcakes and the red-swirl cupcakes, randomly press chocolate chips into the buttercream.

For the mint cupcakes, randomly press in gumdrops. For the cupcakes with the uncolored buttercream, use a skewer to hollow out small holes the size of peas and then spoon a tiny dot of honey into them to replicate toffee. Keep the whipped-ganache cupcakes plain.

Line up the cupcakes on a serving plate in your desired order. Place a sugar cone under the bottom cupcake of each stack, cutting a small slice out of the back of each cone so that it sits flat. Use leftover frosting to stick the cone to the side of the bottom cupcake.

DECORATE THE TOP CUPCAKE OF EACH STACK AS FOLLOWS: For chocolate drips, cut the tip off the piping bag of ganache. Holding the cupcake on its side, pipe along the top edge, letting the drips run across the top of the cupcake. For the sprinkle topping, pour sprinkles onto a small plate and roll the top half of the cupcake in the sprinkles so that they stick to the frosting. Finally, add the Flake bar to the top cupcake of the middle stack.

1 chocolate princess cake (see recipe, page 13)
1 round (8-inch) cake (see recipes, pages 12–13)
1 quantity buttercream (see recipe, page 20)
2 tbsp cocoa powder
food coloring: black
1 cup lollipops or other hard candy
fondant: 9 oz purple, 3 oz green

cornstarch, for rolling out fondant
silver dragées
15 gummy starfish candies
1 Barbie® doll

1 zippered plastic bag
1 straw
1 piping tip (any kind)
metallic food paint (optional)
1 clean paintbrush (optional)
1 rolling pin

STENCIL

Side D: Mermaid Rock &
the Crab Army (fin)

Mermaid Rock & THE CRAB ARMY

TECHNIQUES

Leveling, page 18
Coloring, page 24
Stacking & filling, page 18
Crumb coating, page 18
Creating a smooth finish, page 18
Rolling out fondant, page 21

INSTRUCTIONS

Bake the cakes. Turn them out and leave them to cool completely.

Make the buttercream. Add cocoa powder and black food coloring to color it gray. (Remember the color will intensify as it dries.)

Level the round cake. Place the princess cake back in the pan and use a serrated knife to cut any uneven rising off the bottom of the cake to level it. Turn the princess cake out and place it on top of the round cake. Trim the edges to match. Remove the princess cake again, top the round cake with buttercream, then stack the princess cake back on top. Use a teaspoon to scoop out a center well, wide enough to fit the doll's hips, at the top of the cake. Press the doll's legs down into the center of the cake until her bottom is just sticking out of the cake. Crumb coat the cake with a thin layer of buttercream. Refrigerate the cake until dry to the touch, then place the cake on a serving plate and cover it with buttercream to a smooth finish, reserving a little buttercream for sticking on final details later.

TO MAKE THE CORAL: Put the lollipops in a zippered plastic bag, cover the bag with a kitchen towel, then bang the bag with a rolling pin to break the lollipops into small chunks. Discard the lollipop sticks, then press the lollipop chunks into the buttercream unevenly around the base of the cake to look like coral.

TO MAKE THE MERMAID'S TAIL: Form the purple fondant into a cone about 8 inches long. Make a 1-inch cut in the thick end of the cone, then wrap the cut edges around the doll's hips, joining them at the back to cover her bottom. Arrange the fondant cone in a swirl down the front of the cake.

TO MAKE THE SCALES IN THE TAIL: Use scissors to make a ½-inch-deep slit into one end of the straw, cutting through both sides. Cut off one side of the cut end so that you are left with a semicircular U shape at the end of the straw. Starting at the bottom of the tail, press the U shape into the fondant to make a row of semicircular scales. Continue making rows of scales all the way up the tail, positioning the troughs of every second row of scales above the peaks of the row below.

TO MAKE THE FIN: Trace the fin stencil onto parchment paper and cut it out. Thinly roll out green fondant to a thickness of ⅛ inch, place your stencil on the fondant, and cut out the fin shape. Press the fin into the buttercream at the base of the tail. From the rolled-out green fondant, cut a ½-by-4-inch strip. Wrap the strip around the top of the tail at the doll's waist, tucking the ends into the front of the tail, as shown. Using the wide end of any piping tip, punch 2 circles out of the leftover rolled-out green fondant. Stick the circles to the doll with a spot of water to make a shell bikini top. Use a thin strip of fondant moistened with a little water to make a bikini-top strap that goes around the doll's back. Stick 2 silver dragées, with a small amount of buttercream on them, to the middle of the doll's shell bikini top. Stick a silver dragée to one of the doll's hands, using a tiny dot of leftover buttercream, to make a pearl ring. Use leftover buttercream to stick starfish candies to the cake.

If using metallic food paint, use the paintbrush to paint lines on the fin, waistband, and bikini top, as shown.

The Crab Army Cupcakes continues on page 104 . . .

THE CRAB ARMY CUPCAKES

Bake the cupcakes in the white or silver cupcake wrappers. Turn them out and leave them to cool completely.

Make the royal icing and add it to the piping bag.

Make the buttercream. Add a drop of blue food coloring to it and mix it sparingly to create a marbled effect. Do not overmix it or it will turn one shade of blue.

Messily frost the top of each cupcake to look like textured water. Be careful not to smooth the frosting too much, as you will lose the marbled effect.

TO MAKE THE TURTLES: Cut the spearmint leaves in half lengthwise. Place 4 each of the halved spearmint leaves on 6 of the cupcakes to make the turtles' legs. Cut the tip off the piping bag and stick a peach gummy candy on top of the legs with royal icing. Use the royal icing to attach a green mini gumdrop to the front of each peach gummy candy to form a head. Add 2 white royal-icing eyes to each head.

TO MAKE THE CRABS: Press a gummy fruit wedge, rounded edge down, into the 6 remaining cupcakes. For each fruit wedge, cut a gummy ring of the same color in half. Cut a V out of one end of each ring half and stick it into the buttercream on either side of the fruit wedge, V side up, to make the crabs' pincers. Use royal icing to stick 2 mini gumdrops to the top of each fruit wedge. Pipe a royal-icing eye on each spice drop.

Finally, dip a toothpick into black food coloring and mark a black dot on each of the turtles' and crabs' white eyes.

WHAT YOU NEED

12 cupcakes (see recipes, pages 12–13)
1 quantity royal icing (see recipe, page 20)
1 quantity buttercream (see recipe, page 20)
food colorings: black & blue
12 mini spearmint leaves candy
6 peach gummy candies
6 green mini gumdrops
6 sugared gummy fruit wedges in assorted colors
6 sugared gummy rings in assorted colors
12 mini gumdrops in assorted colors
1 toothpick
1 piping bag
12 plain white or silver cupcake wrappers

THE DANCING TUTUS

The Dancing Tutu Cupcakes continues on page 106 . . .

WHAT YOU NEED

2 round (6-inch) cakes (see recipes, pages 12–13)
1 quantity buttercream (see recipe, page 20)
food coloring: red
1 pink sugar wafer
silver dragées
1 bag pink cotton candy
1 piping bag
1 small star tip (Wilton 30)

TECHNIQUES

Coloring, page 24
Leveling, page 18
Stacking & filling, page 18
Crumb coating, page 18
Creating a smooth finish, page 18
Cutting sugar wafers, page 19

STENCIL

Side D: Swan Lake & the Dancing Tutus (large leotard)

INSTRUCTIONS

Bake the cakes. Turn them out and leave them to cool completely.

Make the buttercream and color it pale pink.

TO MAKE THE LEOTARD: Trace the large leotard stencil onto parchment paper and cut it out. Lay your parchment paper stencil over the pink wafer and, using the tip of a sharp knife, carefully cut out the leotard shape.

Fit the small star tip to the piping bag and fill the piping bag with a couple of spoonfuls of the pink buttercream. Pipe small star shapes around the neck of the leotard, placing a silver dragée in the middle of each star to create the flowers. Pipe a thin line of buttercream around the waist of the leotard and stick on a row of silver dragées.

Level the cakes, then stack and fill them with buttercream. Place the cake on a serving plate, then crumb coat it with a thin layer of buttercream. Refrigerate until dry to the touch. Cover the cake with buttercream to a smooth finish.

Add the cotton-candy tutu and pink-wafer leotard to the cake just before serving, otherwise the cotton candy will dissolve and generally look terrible! Using clean, very dry hands, tear the cotton candy into thin sheets and shape these into a circle about 8 inches in diameter. Once the cotton-candy tutu is in place, make a cut in the center of the cake, through the cotton candy, then press the leotard into the cut so that it stands upright.

The Dancing Tutu Cupcakes continues on page 106 . . .

THE **DANCING TUTU** CUPCAKES

INSTRUCTIONS

Bake the cupcakes in the foil cupcake wrappers and leave them to cool completely.

Make the buttercream and color it pale pink.

TO MAKE THE LEOTARDS: Trace the small leotard stencil onto parchment paper and cut it out. Place your paper stencil on top of a pink wafer and use the tip of a sharp knife to carefully cut out a leotard shape. Repeat with the remaining wafers until you have 12 leotards.

Fit the small star tip to a piping bag, fill the bag with pink buttercream, and squeeze gently to pipe a small star shape on the upper bodice of each leotard. Place a silver dragée in the middle of each star to create a flower.

TO MAKE THE TUTUS: Swap the star tip for the petal tip, then pipe a tutu skirt all the way around each cupcake.

Make a cut down through the frosting and into the center of each cupcake, then press a leotard into each cut so that it stands upright.

Push a row of silver dragées around the waist of each leotard, and into the buttercream of the skirt.

WHAT YOU NEED

12 cupcakes (see recipes, pages 12–13)
½ quantity buttercream (see recipe, page 20)
food coloring: red
12 pink sugar wafers
silver dragées
12 cupcake liners (preferably silver foil)
1 piping bag
1 small star tip (Wilton 30)
1 medium petal tip (Wilton 104)

TECHNIQUES

Coloring, page 24
Piping techniques (tutu skirt), page 29
Cutting sugar wafers, page 19

STENCIL

Side D: Swan Lake & the Dancing Tutus (small leotard)

fondant: 3½ oz white, 3½ oz pale pink & 3½ oz light brown

2 round (6-inch) cakes (see recipes, pages 12–13)

2 round (8-inch) cakes (see recipes, pages 12–13)

2 quantities buttercream with a vegetable shortening base
   (see recipe, page 20)

food colorings: green & red

2 oz white chocolate

silver dragées (small and large sizes; optional)

1 Mentos or large ball-shaped mint

cornstarch, for rolling out fondant

1 round (8-inch) cake board

3 piping bags

10 skewers

6 straws

1 rolling pin

Rolling out fondant, page 21

Coloring, page 24

Melting chocolate, page 19

Leveling, page 18

Crumb coating, page 18

Creating a smooth finish, page 18

Stacking & filling, page 18

Supporting a stack, page 19

Side D: The Galloping Carousel
   (horse & saddle)

THE GALLOPING Carousel

INSTRUCTIONS

TO MAKE THE CAROUSEL HORSES: Make the horses at least a day in advance of serving the cake to allow enough time for them to harden. To make the horses, trace the stencil onto paper and cut it out. Roll out the white fondant to a thickness of ¼ inch. Place your stencil on the fondant and cut out 2 horses and 2 saddles with a sharp knife. Repeat with the pale pink and light brown fondant until you have 2 horses and 2 saddles in each color. Place the shapes on a sheet of parchment paper and, using a small amount of water, stick a white saddle to the back of each brown horse, a pink saddle to the back of each white horse, and a brown saddle to the back of each pink horse, as shown. Set aside in a warm, dry place to harden overnight.

Bake the cakes. Turn them out and leave them to cool completely.

Make the buttercream and divide it among 3 bowls, putting half in 1 bowl and a quarter each in the other 2 bowls. Color the half quantity pale pink, one of the quarter quantities mint green, and keep the remaining quarter quantity white.

TO ATTACH THE HORSES TO THE POLES: Melt the white chocolate. Turn the hardened horses over on the parchment paper and use melted chocolate to stick the middle of the straws onto the horses' backs. Set the carousel horses and the attached rods aside until the chocolate has dried.

TO MAKE THE MIDDLE SECTION OF THE CAROUSEL: Level the 6-inch cakes. Cut a circle with a 4-inch diameter out of parchment paper. Place it on one of the 6-inch leveled cakes and cut around the edge of the parchment paper with a sharp knife to make a cake that is 4 inches in diameter. Repeat this with the second 6-inch cake. Stack and fill the 4-inch round cakes with white buttercream, then crumb coat the stacked cake with a thin layer of white buttercream.

TO MAKE THE BASE OF THE CAROUSEL: Level one of the 8-inch cakes. Crumb coat the leveled 8-inch cake with pink buttercream.

Refrigerate the crumb-coated cakes until dry to the touch.

The Galloping Carousel continues on page 110 . . .

THE GALLOPING
Carousel

CONTINUED

TO MAKE THE ROOF OF THE CAROUSEL: Take the remaining unleveled 8-inch cake and, using the center of the dome as the top point, carve the dome into a steeper slope, as shown, with a serrated knife. Stick this cone-shaped cake to the cake board using a little buttercream. Crumb coat the cake with a thin layer of white buttercream, then refrigerate it until dry to the touch.

Cover the flat 8-inch cake with pale pink buttercream and the 4-inch stacked cake with white buttercream to a smooth finish. Place the 4-inch stack on top of the flat 8-inch cake. Insert a skewer all the way down through the pale pink and white cake stacks and mark the skewer where it enters the cake. Pull out the skewer and cut off above the marked portion with scissors. Using your first skewer as a guide, cut the other 9 skewers to the same height. Push 4 skewers into the white cake so that they are evenly spaced and about ¾ inch in from the edge.

TO ATTACH THE CAROUSEL POLES: Insert the remaining 6 skewers into the pale pink base cake, evenly spacing them, as shown, around the central cake. Slide a straw over each of the outer 6 skewers and push them down into the base cake, arranging them so that the horses are at varying heights. Trim the tops of the straws so they are the same height as the skewers.

TO DECORATE THE CAROUSEL ROOF: Use a knife to mark the carousel roof into 6 equal triangle-shaped portions from apex to rim. Smoothly cover the portions with buttercream, alternating mint green and white. (Don't worry if the edges are a little messy as they will be covered with silver dragées later.) Smoothly cover the rim of the cake with pink buttercream.

Spread buttercream on top of the white center cake and place the carousel roof on top. (The roof will be supported by the skewers and the pole straws.)

Fill a piping bag with leftover mint green buttercream, cut a tiny portion off the tip of the bag, and pipe small dots around the bottom edge of the cake.

Fill a piping bag with leftover pale pink buttercream, cut a tiny portion off the tip of the bag, and pipe small dots along the top edge of both pale pink levels. Push a large silver dragée into every third frosting dot.

Fill a piping bag with leftover white buttercream, cut a tiny portion off the tip of the bag, and pipe a thin line along the divisions between the mint-green and white sections on the roof. Press small silver dragées into the lines of fresh buttercream, spacing them evenly apart.

Finally, use a small amount of white buttercream to attach the Mentos or round mint to the very top of the carousel.

"BIG RED"

WHAT YOU NEED

1 rectangular (9-by-13-inch) cake
(see recipes, pages 12–13)
10 giant yellow licorice allsorts
1 yellow taffy strip
5 oz white chocolate
4 chocolate mint cookies
4 red jelly beans
1 green jelly bean
1 colored saltwater taffy

1 quantity buttercream (see recipe, page 20)
gel food coloring: red
2 x 8-inch (approx.) licorice laces
7 oz Hershey's Giant milk chocolate bar
or a similar large bar
1 licorice or black fondant sheet
2 x 1½-by-5½-inches (approx.) licorice straps
1 piping bag

TECHNIQUES

Melting chocolate, page 19
Coloring, page 24
Leveling, page 18
Stacking & filling, page 18
Crumb coating, page 18
Creating a smooth finish, page 18

STENCILS

Side B: "Big Red" (fire engine, ladder, windows #1 & #2 & windshield)

INSTRUCTIONS

Bake the cake. Turn it out and leave it to cool completely.

Separate the layers of the giant allsorts, gently washing and drying the layers if necessary. Set aside 2 white squares for the control panels. From the remaining white squares, punch out 6 circles with a ¾-inch diameter and 5 circles with a ½-inch diameter (the back end of a standard piping tip is perfect for punching out the 6 larger circles). Cut 2 thin strips from a white allsort square for the windshield wipers. Set the allsort shapes aside.

TO MAKE THE WHEELS: Melt white chocolate and spoon it into a piping bag. Cut a tiny portion off the tip of the bag. Use melted chocolate to stick a ¾-inch white allsort circle to the center of each chocolate mint cookie. Pipe 6 small dots of melted white chocolate around the edge of each wheel, as shown.

TO MAKE THE CONTROL PANELS AND SIREN LIGHTS: Cut jelly beans in half and cut the saltwater taffy in half crosswise. Pipe a dot of melted chocolate to stick a taffy half and half a red and half a green jelly bean to one of the white allsort squares. Repeat this and make a second control panel. For the siren lights, stick half a red jelly bean to each of the ½-inch white allsort circles.

TO MAKE THE HOSE REEL: Pipe a small circle of melted white chocolate on a piece of parchment paper. Roll up a licorice lace into a spiral and press it onto the white chocolate. Hold for a few moments until the licorice is stuck to the chocolate and holds its form. Repeat this and make a second hose reel. To make the hose head, cut 2 small triangles out of the leftover white allsort square and 2 small rectangles out of the yellow allsort leftovers. Use the melted white chocolate to stick first a rectangle then a triangle to the end of each licorice roll, as shown.

"Big Red" continues on page 112 . . .

"BIG RED"

CONTINUED

Make the buttercream and color it red. Level the cake and turn it over. Cut the rectangle into 3 equal widths. Stack and fill the cakes with red buttercream.

Trace the fire engine stencil onto parchment paper and cut it out. Place your stencil against the side of the cake and use a serrated knife to cut out the fire engine shape. Crumb coat the cake with a thin layer of buttercream. Refrigerate the cake until dry to the touch.

Unwrap the block of chocolate and lay it flat, with the smooth side facing up, in the middle of your serving plate. Stick the crumb coated cake to the top of the chocolate block with buttercream. This will hold the fire engine up off the plate. Cover the cake with buttercream to a smooth finish.

TO MAKE THE WINDOWS AND WINDSHIELD: Trace the windows and windshield stencils onto parchment paper and cut them out. Use your stencils to cut the shapes out of the sheet of licorice, then set them in place on the cab of the fire engine, pressing them into the buttercream. Stick on the allsort windshield wipers (made earlier) with melted white chocolate.

Push the 4 chocolate mint cookie wheels into the buttercream on the sides of the fire engine.

Cut 4 long, thin strips out of the yellow taffy strip and press them into the buttercream on the front of the cake to make a grille.

Press the 2 remaining ¾-inch white circles into the buttercream on either side of the grille for the headlights. Out of the rest of the yellow allsort layers, cut ¾-inch-long diamond shapes. Press the diamonds into the buttercream on an angle in a line around the middle of the fire engine just below the windows. Press a hose reel and a control panel into the buttercream on each side of the engine. Place the half jelly-bean siren lights in a line on the top of the cab.

TO MAKE THE LADDERS: Trace the ladder stencil onto parchment paper and cut it out. Using your stencil as a guide and cutting with the tip of a very sharp knife, cut small, evenly spaced rectangles out of the 2 licorice straps to make rungs for the ladders. Place the ladders on either side of the roof, inserting the front of each ladder into the buttercream of the cab to hold it upright.

THE DIRTY DIGGER

WHAT YOU NEED

1 rectangular (9-by-13-inch) chocolate cake
  (see recipe, page 13)

½ quantity milk chocolate ganache (see recipe, page 21)

1 quantity buttercream (see recipe, page 20)

food coloring: yellow

1½ cups dark chocolate chips

1 x 3½-oz thin dark chocolate bar

6 x 1½-oz packages Kit Kat bars (24 wafers)

1 piping bag

1 palette knife or offset spatula

TECHNIQUES

Coloring, page 24

Melting chocolate, page 19

Leveling, page 18

Stacking and filling, page 18

Crumb coating, page 18

Creating a smooth finish, page 18

STENCILS

Side B: The Dirty Digger (cab & body, for reference; grille,
  left wheel, right wheel, window & windshield)

INSTRUCTIONS

Bake the cake. Turn it out and leave it to cool completely. Make the ganache and set it aside to firm up. Make the buttercream and color it bright yellow.

Place a sheet of parchment paper on a flat surface. Melt the dark chocolate chips and spread the melted chocolate thinly on the paper with a palette knife or offset spatula. Refrigerate the chocolate until set. Trace the window (including windshield) and grille stencils onto paper and cut them out. Once the chocolate has set hard, lay your window and grille stencils on top of it. Pour boiling water into a cup and stand a sharp knife in the cup for 30 seconds to heat it up. Dry the hot knife, then cut around the window and grille shapes, reheating and drying the knife when necessary.

TO MAKE THE DIGGER BUCKET: Break off 2 rows of 2 squares each of the thin chocolate bar. Set the squares aside. Break off another square and cut it in half diagonally. Melt the remaining chocolate, spoon it into the piping bag, and cut a tiny portion off the tip of the bag. Use melted chocolate to glue the long edges of the 2 rows of chocolate together at a right angle, holding them momentarily until the chocolate hardens, then use more melted chocolate to glue on the 2 triangle halves at either end of the bucket, again holding the pieces until the chocolate hardens. Set the bucket aside to dry. Use the remaining melted chocolate to pipe cross-hatching on the chocolate grill.

Level the cake. Save the cake offcut for crumbling into dirt. Cut the cake into 4 equal widths.

TO MAKE THE BODY OF THE DIGGER: Stack and fill 2 widths of cake with buttercream. To make the cab of the digger, cut the third width of cake in half, then stack and fill it. Stack and fill the cab to one end of the digger body. Crumb coat the cake with a thin layer of yellow buttercream. Refrigerate the cake until dry to the touch. Place the cake on your serving plate, then cover it with buttercream to a smooth finish (it will need to be a thick layer to cover the dark chocolate cake). Place the chocolate windows and grill on the digger, pressing them into the buttercream.

Separate the Kit Kat bars into single wafers. Put 2 whole wafers aside, then cut the remaining wafers in half. Trace the digger wheel stencils onto parchment paper and cut out stencils. Place your stencils on the remaining width of cake and cut out 2 triangle-shaped wheels. Cover the wheels with ganache. Press the Kit Kat half-lengths into the ganache along the base of each wheel. Pick up the wheels and press them, base side down, into the buttercream on either side of the digger. Continue pressing Kit Kat half-lengths around the wheels until they are completely covered.

TO MAKE THE HEADLIGHTS: Cut small cubes out of 2 leftover Kit Kat wafers and stick them on top of the digger's body with a little buttercream.

TO MAKE THE BUCKET ARMS: Place the digger bucket in front of the digger and press 2 leftover Kit Kat wafers into the buttercream, as shown.

TO MAKE THE DIRT: Crumble the cake offcuts in and around the digger bucket.

1 round (6-inch) cake (see recipes, pages 12–13)

1 round (8-inch) cake (see recipes, pages 12–13)

2 quantities buttercream with vegetable shortening base (see recipe, page 20)

food colorings: black & blue

2 piping bags

1 basket-weave tip (Wilton 47)

1 medium round tip (Wilton 4)

4 skewers

4 straws

1 balloon

1 tea-light candle

UP, UP & AWAY

TECHNIQUES

Coloring, page 24

Leveling, page 18

Crumb coating, page 18

Creating a smooth finish, page 18

Piping techniques (basket weave & rope), page 30

INSTRUCTIONS

Bake the cakes. Turn them out and leave them to cool completely.

Make the buttercream with a vegetable shortening base. Place 3 heaped tablespoons of uncolored buttercream in a piping bag and set the bag aside. Halve the remaining buttercream and color one half light blue and the other gray.

Level the 8-inch cake. Crumb coat the cake with a thin layer of light blue buttercream, then refrigerate it until dry to the touch.

Cut a circle with a 4-inch diameter out of parchment paper. Level the 6-inch cake and place the parchment paper circle on top. Cut around the edge of the parchment paper with a sharp knife to make a 4-inch cake round. Crumb coat the cake with a thin layer of gray buttercream, then refrigerate it until dry to the touch.

Place the 8-inch cake on a serving plate. Cover the cake with the light blue buttercream to a smooth finish. Cover only the top of the 4-inch cake with gray buttercream to a smooth finish, retaining enough buttercream for the basket-weave piping. Place the gray cake on the center of the blue cake.

TO MAKE THE CLOUDS: Cut a ¼–½-inch portion off the tip of the piping bag containing uncolored buttercream and pipe fluffy white cloud shapes around the outside of the blue base.

TO MAKE THE BASKET: Fill a piping bag with gray buttercream and pipe a basket-weave pattern all around the sides of the gray cake. Change to a medium round tip. Pipe the rope pattern around the rim of the basket.

Push 4 skewers, spaced evenly and angled slightly outward, through the gray basket and down into the blue cake. The angle of the skewers creates a big cradle for the balloon. Slide the straws over the skewers.

Just before serving the cake, blow up the balloon and rest it in between the straws. Place a tea-light candle on the basket cake, under the balloon, as shown. Only light the candle immediately before serving, as the heat from the flame will pop the balloon if left for too long!

THE CHOO CHOO TRAIN

WHAT YOU NEED

2 rectangular (9-by-13-inch) cakes
  (see recipes, pages 12–13)
2 quantities buttercream (see recipe, page 20)
food colorings: blue & yellow
gel food coloring: red
11 giant licorice allsorts
18 Oreo cookies
8 x 8-inch (approx.) licorice ribbons
15 (approx.) white mini marshmallows
6 oz sprinkle-coated licorice gumdrops

20 candy-coated round chocolate candies
8 x 8-inch (approx.) licorice laces
3½ ft (approx.) licorice straps
3 short licorice sticks
1 can cutter (see page 17)
3 piping bags
3 large round tips (Wilton 6) or use 1 tip and
  wash it between colors
1 x 4-inch-length white floral wire
toothpicks

STENCILS

Side B: The Choo Choo Train
  (cab, car, chimney & engine)

TECHNIQUES

Leveling, page 18
Crumb coating, page 18
Stacking & filling, page 18
Creating a smooth finish, page 18

INSTRUCTIONS

Bake the cakes. Turn them out and leave to cool completely.

Make the buttercream. Divide it evenly among 3 bowls and color 1 yellow, 1 blue, and 1 red.

Separate the layers of 3 giant allsorts. Gently wash the black licorice layers with a little water if necessary and set them aside on a paper towel to dry.

Level the cake. Trace the train stencils onto parchment paper and cut them out. Place your stencils on the cake and cut out 6 car rectangles, 1 engine shape, and 2 cab squares. Use the can cutter to punch out 3 circles from the leftover cake. Cut 1 small cylinder of cake 1¼ inches in diameter for the chimney (or use the chimney stencil as your guide).

TO MAKE THE CARS: Separate the 6 rectangles of cake for the cars into 3 stacks, each 2 rectangles high. Fill and stack each with a different-colored buttercream. Crumb coat the cars with the matching buttercream, then refrigerate them until dry to the touch.

TO MAKE THE CAB AND ENGINE: Stack the 2 cab squares of cake at the back of the engine cake with blue buttercream. Use a sharp serrated knife to carve the point at the front of the engine car into a slope, as shown. Crumb coat the sides of both the engine and the cab in blue buttercream and the rest of the engine and the cab in red buttercream, as shown. Refrigerate the engine and cab until dry to the touch.

Fill and stack the 3 large round cake cylinders with yellow buttercream, then cut ¼ inch off one curved edge to make a flat base for the stacked cylinder to sit on. Crumb coat the cylinder in yellow buttercream. Crumb coat the smaller cylinder cake in red buttercream, then refrigerate both cylinder cakes until dry to the touch.

Remove all the cakes from the fridge. Cover them with buttercream to a smooth finish, matching the colors of the crumb coating. (Don't worry if the edges are not perfect—they will be piped over later.)

Place the flat side of the yellow cylinder on the front of the engine car, as shown. Use a sharp knife and a spoon to make a ½ inch deep by 1½ inches round hole in the top of the yellow cylinder and place the chimney in the hole. Put the remainder of each color of buttercream in a separate piping bag fitted with large round tips and cut a tiny portion off the tip of each bag. Pipe a line of red buttercream around the roofline of the cab and along the sides of the yellow engine, hiding the join between the two frosting colors. On the sloped point of the engine car, pipe a grille with red buttercream.

TO MAKE THE WHEELS: Stick 3 Oreos down each side of the engine car and pipe a small dot of blue buttercream in the center of each. Trim 2 licorice ribbons to 7 inches and stick them across the buttercream dots on the Oreos to connect the wheels.

Stick 4 squares of the black licorice allsort layers on each side of the cab to make big square windows. To make the smoke, bend floral wire into a gentle curve and thread mini marshmallows onto one end. Insert the clear end of the floral wire through the chimney and down into the engine of the cake.

On the long sides of the red car, pipe a red box around the edges and an X across the middle. Stick 2 Oreo wheels to the buttercream on each side of the car and pipe a red dot in the center of each wheel. Repeat this process with the other 2 cars, using the yellow, then the blue buttercream. Form a tray around the edge of each car by pressing lengths of licorice ribbon into the buttercream. Pile licorice gel drops and chocolate candies into each car tray, using buttercream to hold them in place.

TO MAKE THE TRACKS: On a flat plate, board, or serving area, make the tracks by positioning the rest of the wide licorice straps in two large arcs about 3 inches apart. (Stick the licorice to the board with a small amount of buttercream if necessary.) Cut the 8 licorice laces in half and place them at even intervals across the tracks.

TO ASSEMBLE THE TRAIN: Place the engine car at the front of the train tracks with all the cars lined up behind it. Push a toothpick through the center of each short licorice stick so the toothpick sticks out at each end. Join the cars together by inserting the ends of the toothpick logs into each cake.

Rainbow's END

WHAT YOU NEED

1 round (10-inch) cake (see recipes, pages 12–13)
1 quantity buttercream (see recipe, page 20)
food coloring: blue
fondant: 7 oz white, 3½ oz red, 3 oz orange,
  2¾ oz yellow, 2½ oz light green, 2 oz light blue,
  1¾ oz indigo & 1½ oz violet
cornstarch, for rolling out fondant
1 rolling pin

TECHNIQUES

Coloring, page 24
Leveling, page 18
Crumb coating, page 18
Rolling out fondant, page 21
Creating a smooth finish, page 18

INSTRUCTIONS

Bake the cake. Turn it out and leave it to cool completely.

Make the buttercream and color it light blue.

Level the cake, then cut it in half from the top down, right across its diameter. Spread buttercream on one of the semicircle surfaces, sandwich the semicircles together, and stand the sandwiched cake up on its side. Crumb coat the cake with a thin layer of buttercream, then refrigerate it until dry to the touch.

TO MAKE THE CLOUDS: Form 15–20 small, irregularly sized balls, ranging from pea-sized to marble-sized, out of white fondant. Randomly stack the balls into 2 cloud shapes, sticking them together with a spot of water. Thinly roll out the remaining white fondant to a thickness of ⅛ inch, and big enough to cover each cloud shape. Mold the piece of fondant around each cloud, pushing it into all the nooks and crevices to create a smooth, contoured cloud. Tuck any excess fondant underneath.

TO MAKE THE RAINBOW: Using your hands, roll out all the remaining fondant colors into 16-inch-long ropes with a diameter of ½ inch. Using your cake pan as a guide, cut out a 10-inch round piece of parchment paper. Fold the paper in half to make a semicircle. Lay the roll of red fondant around the top curved edge of the semicircle, so that it extends just below the flat edge. Place the orange rope inside the red, then add the yellow, green, blue, indigo, and violet ropes. Using a sharp knife, trim the ends of the rainbow so that they match at each end.

Place the cake on the serving dish, then cover it with buttercream to a smooth finish, setting a small amount aside for securing the clouds. Remove the fondant ropes from the parchment paper, starting with the violet rope at the bottom, and press them into the semicircular face of the cake one at a time.

Use a little buttercream to secure one cloud at each end of the rainbow.

LOST *in* SPACE

WHAT YOU NEED

2 round (6-inch) cakes (see recipes, pages 12–13)

2 round (8-inch) cakes (see recipes, pages 12–13)

2 quantities buttercream or ganache (see recipes, pages 20–21)

fondant: 3 lb navy blue, 3½ oz white, 3½ oz red, 1¾ oz light blue, 1¾ oz orange, 1¾ oz green, 1 oz choice of color for skin (peach shown), 1 oz gray, 1 oz dark gray, ⅓ oz light purple & ⅓ oz dark purple

cornstarch, for rolling out fondant

silver dragées

5 dowels or skewers

1 rolling pin

1 fondant smoother

1 round (6-inch) cake board

TECHNIQUES

Rolling out fondant, page 21

Leveling, page 18

Stacking & filling, page 18

Creating a smooth finish, page 18

Covering a cake with fondant, page 23

Supporting a stack, page 19

STENCILS

Side D: Lost in Space (astronaut, planets x 2 & rocket)

INSTRUCTIONS

Make the fondant astronaut, rocket, and planets at least a day in advance of serving the cake to allow for drying time. Trace the stencils onto parchment paper and cut them out. Thinly roll out the assorted colors of fondant to a thickness of ⅛ inch and, using your stencils, cut out the shapes. Use a spot of water between the layers of fondant to stick different-colored details together, using the picture as a guide. Lay the shapes on parchment paper or a silicone sheet until firm and dry enough to pick up.

Bake the cakes. Turn them out and leave them to cool completely.

Make the buttercream or ganache.

Level the cakes. Stack and fill the 8-inch cakes with buttercream or ganache, then cover the cake stack in buttercream or ganache to a smooth finish. Place the 8-inch cake stack on a serving plate and set aside.

Repeat this process for the 6-inch cakes, then stick the 6-inch cake stack to a 6-inch cake board using a small amount of buttercream or ganache.

Roll out 1¾ lb navy blue fondant to a thickness of ¼ inch, and approximately 16 inches in diameter. Place the fondant over the 8-inch cake, then smooth and trim it.

Repeat this process for the 6-inch cake, this time rolling out 21 oz navy blue fondant to a thickness of ¼ inch and a diameter of 14 inches. Place the fondant over the 6-inch cake, then smooth and trim it.

Use the dowels or skewers to support and stack the cakes together.

Push the dragées randomly into the navy blue fondant, while it is still soft, to make stars.

Dot the undersides of the astronaut, rocket, and planet shapes with buttercream or ganache, then attach them to the sides of the cake.

Frank the ROBOT

WHAT YOU NEED

3 rectangular (9-by-13-inch) cakes (see recipes, pages 12–13)
1 quantity royal icing (see recipe, page 20)
food colorings: black, blue, red & yellow
2 round candy-coated chocolate candies
1 licorice sheet or black fondant
12 orange giant licorice allsorts
1 taffy strip
2 quantities buttercream (see recipe, page 20)
3 jelly beans in different colors

12 small licorice allsorts:
   1 green, 9 orange, 1 pink & 1 yellow
2 Oreo cookies
1 short licorice stick
8 skewers
1 square (4-by-4-inch) cake board
toothpicks
1 x 8-inch-length white floral wire
2 straws

TECHNIQUES

Coloring, page 24; Leveling, page 18; Crumb coating, page 18; Stacking & filling, page 18; Creating a smooth finish, page 18

INSTRUCTIONS

Bake the cakes. Turn them out and leave them to cool completely.

Make the royal icing and color it orange.

TO MAKE THE ANTENNAE: Use the tip of a sharp knife to carefully "drill" a small hole in each candy-coated chocolate candy, then push the sharp end of a skewer into each hole. Holding the skewers, dip each candy-coated chocolate candy into the orange royal icing until completely coated, then set the antennae aside in a glass to dry.

TO MAKE THE CONTROL PANEL: Cut the licorice sheet into a rectangle about 3 by 4½ inches. Separate the layers of 2 giant licorice allsorts, gently and briefly washing the layers in water if necessary, then setting them aside on a paper towel to dry. You will have 6 black squares, 4 orange squares, and 4 white squares. Cut a circle out of 1 orange square and then a triangle out of the middle of that circle. Place 2 white squares side-by-side

and cut out 1 semicircle. Cut 2 white strips from the leftover white squares. Cut 3 narrow slices from the taffy strip. Cut 3 jelly beans in half. From a black licorice allsort square, cut a small arrow that is ¾ inch long. Using the picture as a guide, arrange all these candies on the licorice rectangle and attach them with royal icing. Set the control panel aside to dry.

TO MAKE THE ARMS: Stack 2 giant licorice allsorts on top of each other and hold them together by pushing a toothpick through the center of them, leaving ¼ inch of toothpick sticking out below. Repeat this process for the second arm. From the leftover orange squares, cut out 2 rings (make circles and cut out their centers). Attach the ring shapes to the end of each arm by pushing the tip of the toothpick into the edge of the orange ring. Make a cut through the bottom half of each ring to create pincers.

Make the buttercream and color it dusty blue.

Frank the Robot continues on page 128 . . .

Frank THE ROBOT

CONTINUED

TO MAKE THE BODY AND HEAD: Level the cakes and turn them over. Cut the cakes into 4 squares measuring 6 by 6 inches each. Stack and fill the cakes with buttercream. From the leftover cake, cut 3 squares measuring 4 by 4 inches. Stack and fill the cakes with buttercream. Stick the 4-inch stack onto a 4-by-4-inch cake board with a little buttercream. Crumb coat both cake stacks with a thin layer of buttercream, then refrigerate the cakes until dry to the touch. Place the large cake on a serving plate and cover it with buttercream to a smooth finish.

TO MAKE THE NECK: In the center of the top of the large cake arrange 9 small orange licorice allsorts into a square 3 by 3 candies wide. Push a skewer through the middle of each corner orange licorice allsort, right down into the large stacked cake. Cut the top of the 4 skewers flush with the top of the licorice allsorts. Spread buttercream on top of the licorice allsort square and place the small square cake on top. Cover this cake with buttercream to a smooth finish.

TO MAKE THE LEGS: Stack 3 giant licorice allsorts together and push them onto the end of a skewer. Repeat this process for the second leg. Insert the leg skewers into the front of the large cake, as shown.

Use royal icing to stick the control panel to the front of the robot, holding it in place for a moment until it sticks.

TO ATTACH THE ARMS: Push a toothpick sideways into the top licorice allsort, then push the other end of the toothpick into the side of the large cake, ring pincer facing downward. Repeat this process with the other arm on the other side of the cake.

TO MAKE THE EYES: Twist apart 2 Oreo cookies, discarding the side of each cookie that has no filling on it. Cut 2 thin slices off the short licorice stick and stick 1 to the icing side of each Oreo, using royal icing. The specific placement of the licorice slices gives the eyes personality, so practice on paper first if you like. Attach the eyes to the head with royal icing.

TO MAKE THE TEETH AND LIPS: Cut a thin slice off each of the green, pink, and yellow licorice allsorts. Attach them to the head in a line, using royal icing. Cut slices from the leftover black licorice sheet for lips and press them into the buttercream around the teeth, as shown.

TO ASSEMBLE THE ANTENNAE: Bend the floral wire into random zigzags until the wire is approximately 3½ inches in length. Wrap the ends of the wire around the top of the skewers directly under the orange-colored chocolate candies. Cut the straws down to 2½ inches and slip them over the skewers. Push the ends of the skewers into the robot's head.

WHAT YOU NEED

1 quantity gingerbread (see recipe, page 14)

2 round (10-inch) cakes (see recipes, pages 12–13)

1 quantity royal icing (see recipe, page 20)

3 pink sugar wafers

1 quantity buttercream (see recipe, page 20)

food coloring: green

4½ cups shredded coconut

50 (approx.) multicolored white chocolate nonpareils

6 gummy heart candies

1 Wonka Nerds Rope

1 x 1½-oz Kit Kat bar (4 wafers)

¼ cup Skittles

2 round (2-inches approx.) lollipops

1 large round (3-inches approx.) lollipop

2 white chocolate disks

2 gumdrops

6 coconut-coated gumdrops or similar

11 flower-shaped candies in different colors

2 piping bags

1 small round tip (Wilton 3)

1 zippered plastic bag

toothpicks

STENCILS

Side B: Home Sweet Home (door, front & back wall, side wall, roof, shutter, window & picket)

TECHNIQUES

Coloring, page 24

Leveling, page 18

Stacking & filling, page 18

Crumb coating, page 18

Creating a smooth finish, page 18

Coloring coconut, page 19

Cutting sugar wafers, page 19

INSTRUCTIONS

Make the gingerbread pieces in advance and store them in an airtight container in the fridge for up to a week. Make the gingerbread dough, then roll it out on a floured surface to a thickness of ¼–½ inch. Trace the door, front & back wall, side wall, roof, shutter, window & picket stencils onto parchment paper and cut them out. Place your stencils on the dough and use the point of a sharp knife to cut out 2 roof pieces, 2 side walls, 2 front walls, and 30 pickets. Lay out all the gingerbread pieces on a baking sheet lined with parchment paper and place the tray in the fridge or freezer for 10–15 minutes. (This helps the gingerbread pieces to hold their shape during baking.) Bake the gingerbread, then leave it to cool completely.

Bake the cakes. Turn them out and leave them to cool completely.

TO ASSEMBLE THE HOUSE: Make the royal icing. Spoon it into a piping bag and cut a small portion off the tip of the bag. Stick the 4 walls together, using plenty of royal icing. To keep the walls upright while the royal icing dries, stand cups on either side of the walls for support. When the walls are stable, but not necessarily dry, pipe royal icing along the top edge of the walls and attach the roof pieces. Pipe a line of royal icing along the apex of the roof to join the pieces. Leave the house to dry.

Home Sweet Home continues on page 130 . . .

HOME
sweet
HOME

Fit a small round tip onto the second piping bag and fill it with royal icing. Pipe a thin outline around each picket and set them aside to dry.

TO MAKE THE DOOR, WINDOWS & SHUTTERS: Cut a pink wafer into a 1½-by-3-inch rectangle (or use the door stencil as your guide) and use the royal icing to pipe on the door pattern, as shown. From the remaining pink wafers, cut 2 squares measuring 1½ by 1½ inches (or use the window stencil as your guide) and 4 rectangles measuring ¾ by 1½ inches (or use the shutter stencil as your guide). Pipe window panes on the squares and horizontal lines on the rectangle shutters as shown. Set the door, windows, and shutters aside to dry.

Make the buttercream and color it green. Level the cakes, then stack and fill them with buttercream. Place the cake on a serving plate, then cover it with buttercream to a smooth finish. Color the coconut green. Press the green coconut grass into the buttercream until the cake is completely covered.

Use royal icing to evenly stick the gingerbread pickets around the cake, leaving a 3-inch gap at the front of the cake for the path.

TO DECORATE THE HOUSE: Once the gingerbread house is sturdy enough to move, carefully place it at the back of the cake. To tile the roof, use royal icing to stick on overlapping layers of chocolate nonpareils, starting from the bottom of each roof side. Stick gummy hearts in between the chocolate nonpareils along the peak of the roof. Stick the Wonka Nerds Rope along the front of the roof using royal icing. Use leftover white chocolate nonpareils to make a path from the front of the house to the gate. Use royal icing to stick the door to the front of the house and a window to each side. Stick a shutter, on an angle, as shown, on either side of the windows. For the planter boxes, break 2 wafers off the Kit Kat bar and use royal icing to stick 1 wafer below each window (support the Kit Kat bar with toothpicks while the royal icing dries). Stick Skittles above the front door in a flower shape. Push the 2-inch lollipops into the cake on either side of the door and the larger lollipop through one of the roof panels as a chimney.

TO MAKE THE FLOWERPOTS: Use royal icing to stick a gumdrop to the flat side of a chocolate disk, then top the spice drop with a flower candy. Make a second flowerpot, then place the flowerpots at either side of the door. Push the coconut-coated gumdrops into the grass on the sides of the house. Arrange the flower candies on the grass and in the planter boxes, sticking them on with royal icing if necessary.

WHAT YOU NEED

1 quantity royal icing (see recipe, page 20)

1 sheet rice paper or wafer paper (wafer paper is sold at cake-decorating stores)

edible glitter (optional)

1 butterfly-shaped sprinkle

1 chocolate princess cake (see recipe, page 13)

1 round (8-inch) cake (see recipes, pages 12–13)

1 quantity buttercream (see recipe, page 20)

food coloring: green

silver dragées

80–90 giant spearmint leaves candy

1 piping bag

1 medium round tip (Wilton 4)

1 x 3-inch-length white floral wire

1 Barbie® doll

TECHNIQUES

Coloring, page 24

Leveling, page 18

Creating a smooth finish, page 18

INSTRUCTIONS

Make the royal icing. Fit the medium round tip to the piping bag and fill it with uncolored royal icing.

TO MAKE THE FAIRY WINGS: Trace the wings stencil, including all the spiral patterns, onto paper and cut it out. Place your stencil on rice or wafer paper, trace the outline of the wings and cut them out. Now place the rice or wafer-paper wings on top of your paper stencil and pipe the spiral design onto the wings with royal icing. Lay the wings on a flat surface to dry, weighing down the middle of the wings with a spoon so the wings don't curl up. If you're using edible glitter, sprinkle it over the wings while the royal icing is still wet.

TO MAKE THE WAND: Glue the butterfly-shaped sprinkle to one end of the floral wire with royal icing. Set it aside on parchment paper to dry.

Bake the cakes. Turn them out and leave them until completely cool.

Make the buttercream and color it mint green.

SYLVIE
THE
Fairy Leaf
PRINCESS

STENCIL

Side D: Sylvie the Fairy Leaf Princess (wings)

Level the round cake. Place the princess cake back in the pan and use a serrated knife to cut any uneven rising off the cake to level it, then turn the cake out. Place the princess cake on top of the round cake and trim the edges of the cakes to match. Separate the cakes, cover the top of the round cake with buttercream, then place the princess cake back on top.

Use a teaspoon to scoop out a well in the center of the top of the cake. It needs to be wide enough to fit the doll's hips. Press the doll's legs down into the center of the cake so that she is visible only from her belly button up. Cover the cake with buttercream to a smooth finish. Extend the buttercream up over the torso to make a bodice with a heart-shaped neckline. Pipe small dots of royal icing along the top of the bodice and place a small silver dragée in the center.

TO MAKE THE SKIRT: Starting at the bottom of the cake, attach rows of giant spearmint leaves around the cake (use some royal icing as glue if the leaves are not sticking to the buttercream). Continue layering the leaves all the way to the top of the skirt, placing every alternating row of leaves above the gullies created by the row below.

Randomly select a leaf on the skirt and pipe 5 small dots in a circle on it with royal icing. Push a silver dragée into the center of the circle to make a small flower. Pipe more of these flowers randomly all over the skirt.

When the wand is dry, wrap the end of the wire around one of the doll's hands.

When the details on the wings are dry, use a spot of royal icing to stick the wings to the doll's back, underneath her hair.

The Magic Kingdom

WHAT YOU NEED

2 round (6-inch) cakes (see recipes, pages 12–13)

2 round (8-inch) cakes (see recipes, pages 12–13)

1 quantity royal icing (see recipe, page 20)

food coloring: red

9 flat-based standard ice cream cones (see page 19)

1 cup pink sugar sprinkles

2 quantities buttercream (see recipe, page 20)

5 pointed standard ice cream cones (see page 19)

6 cups mini marshmallows

1 pink sugar wafer

2 silver dragées

1 pastry brush

1 round (6-inch) cake board

6 dowels or skewers

TECHNIQUES

Coloring, page 24

Leveling, page 18

Stacking & filling, page 18

Supporting a stack, page 19

Creating a smooth finish, page 18

INSTRUCTIONS

Bake the cakes. Turn them out and leave them to cool completely. Make the royal icing and color it pale pink.

TO MAKE THE TURRETS: Use a pastry brush to paint the pink royal icing over the outside of the flat-based cones. Press 2 cones together, base to base, to make 4 pairs, leaving 1 cone unattached. Set the cones aside to dry, standing them upright.

Pour the pink sugar sprinkles into a shallow bowl. Spread the royal icing over the pointed standard cones, roll the cones in pink sugar sprinkles, and set them aside to dry, standing them upright. Once the cones are dry, attach a cone to the top of each turret, as well as to the unattached cone, with a little royal icing. Set the cones aside to dry.

Make the buttercream and color it pink. Level the cakes. Stack and fill the 8-inch cakes with buttercream, then stack and fill the 6-inch cakes with buttercream. Stick the 6-inch cake stack to the 6-inch cake board using buttercream. Stack the 6-inch tier on top of the 8-inch tier using 5 dowels or skewers as supports.

Cover the cake with buttercream to a smooth finish. Press the 4 tall cone turrets into the buttercream around the base of the cake. Press mini marshmallows into the buttercream in a brick pattern all the way up the sides of the cakes, using royal icing as glue if necessary.

TO MAKE THE BATTLEMENTS: Press a row of mini marshmallows around the top edge of both tiers, leaving even gaps in between.

Stick 1 dowel or a skewer through the bottom of the shortest cone turret and use the skewer to anchor it to the top of the cake stack.

TO MAKE THE DOOR: Cut the top two corners off the pink sugar wafer to form an arch shape. Stick the door to the front of the cake with royal icing. To make the door handles, stick 2 silver dragées to the middle of the door with royal icing.

1 x 3-oz package blue Jell-O

2 quantities white chocolate ganache (see recipe, page 21)

2 rectangular (9-by-13-inch) cakes
  (see recipes, pages 12–13)

18 oz dark chocolate

8 flat-based standard ice cream cones (see page 19)

3 pointed standard ice cream cones (see page 19)

1 quantity royal icing (see recipe, page 20)

gel food coloring: green (or combine blue & yellow)

34 oz mini Charleston Chews

1 x 1½-oz Kit Kat bar (4 wafers)

2 chocolate Pirouette cookies

2 orange giant licorice allsorts

1 pastry brush

1 can cutter (see page 17)

1 piping bag

1 grass tip (Wilton 233)

3 toothpicks

Old KING COLE'S Castle

TECHNIQUES

Melting chocolate, page 19; Leveling, page 18;
Stacking & filling, page 18; Crumb coating, page 18;
Creating a smooth finish, page 18

INSTRUCTIONS

Make the blue Jell-O the day before, according to the packet's instructions. Pour it into a shallow baking pan and refrigerate it until set. Make the white chocolate ganache and set it aside to firm up. Bake the cakes. Turn them out and leave until completely cool.

TO MAKE THE TURRETS: Melt the dark chocolate, then dip the outsides of all the ice cream cones in the melted chocolate until they are completely coated. Stand pointed cones upside down to dry. Stack flat-based cones base to base to create 4 separate turrets. Stand them on parchment paper and allow to dry. Re-melt chocolate and use a pastry brush to paint inside one end of each flat-based cone turret. Set the cones aside to dry.

Level the cakes, then cut the 2 rectangles down to 2 equal-sized squares. Save the offcuts, as you'll use them later. Stack and fill the cakes with ganache. Use the can cutter to shape the bottom corners of the cake so that the cone turrets slot into them. Stick the 4 turrets to the cake with ganache. Crumb coat the cake with a thin layer of ganache, then refrigerate the cake until ganache is dry to the touch.

TO MAKE THE TOWERS: Use a can cutter to punch 6 circles out of the cake offcuts. Stack and fill with ganache to make 1-layer, 2-layer, and 3-layer cake stacks. Crumb coat the cake stacks with a thin layer of ganache and refrigerate them until dry to the touch.

Place the square cake on the serving plate. Make the royal icing, then divide it evenly between 2 bowls. Color 1 bowl light green and the other a darker green by adding more gel. Fit the grass tip to the piping bag and fill the bag with 1 shade of green. All around the edge of the serving plate randomly pipe blobs of

icing while pulling up and away from the cake to make grass. Leave gaps for the second shade of green. Refill the piping bag with the second shade of green and complete the grass border, making sure you leave enough space for your Jell-O moat.

Cover the cake with ganache to a smooth finish. Press mini Charleston Chews chocolate candies in a horizontal brick pattern into the sides of the cake, leaving a 2½-inches-wide gap in the middle of the front wall for your drawbridge. Use a sharp knife to cut the chocolates to fit around the turrets on the corners of the cake and press them in place to complete the brick-patterned walls. Then cut the chocolates in half to make battlements along the top edge of the walls. Use a little ganache to stick the battlements, cut side down, to the top of the chocolate brick wall, leaving equal-sized gaps in between. Lay the Kit Kat bar in front of the drawbridge gap. Use ganache to affix the chocolate Pirouettes to the cake and the drawbridge.

Cover the round cake stacks with ganache to a smooth finish and press Charleston Chews around them horizontally in a brick pattern. Top the cake stacks with battlements made from halved chocolates. Arrange the towers on the square cake.

TO MAKE THE ORANGE FLAGS: Carefully peel apart the layers of the giant licorice allsorts. Cut 3 triangles out of the orange layers and insert the end of a toothpick into each. Push the other end of each toothpick into a pointy chocolate cone. Place each pointed cone with a flag on a cake tower.

Just before serving, carefully spoon Jell-O into the moat space between the castle and the royal icing grass.

Guitar LESSONS

TECHNIQUES

Melting chocolate, page 19
Coloring, page 24
Leveling, page 18
Crumb coating, page 18
Creating a smooth finish, page 18

INSTRUCTIONS

Make the ganache and set it aside to firm up. Bake the cake. Turn it out and leave it to cool completely.

TO MAKE THE TUNING PEGS: Slice 6 x ¼-inch pieces from the licorice twist. Slice the licorice sticks into 6 flat disks. Melt the chocolate and use it to stick the licorice twist pieces to each disk. Set the pegs aside to dry.

TO MAKE THE NECK OF THE GUITAR: Using the melted chocolate as glue, stick vanilla sugar wafers together end to end and make a stack that is 4 wafers long, 3 wafers high, and 2 wafers wide. To make the head of the guitar, stick a row of 3 wafers on top of one end of the neck, evenly spacing the wafers across so that the head of the guitar is centered over the thinner neck. Add another layer of wafer biscuits all the way down the neck of the guitar so that the head and neck are level. Using a sharp serrated knife cut the corners off the head on a diagonal. Stick 3 licorice tuning pegs to each side of the head, using melted chocolate.

Make the buttercream, then add cocoa powder and food colorings to it to make it light brown. Level the cake and turn it over. Trace the guitar body stencil onto parchment paper and cut it out. Place your stencil on the cake and cut out the guitar shape. Using a spoon and the stencil as a guide, scoop out a ¾-inch-deep circular sound hole in the guitar.

Crumb coat the cake with a thin layer of ganache. Refrigerate the cake until dry to the touch. Place the guitar body on a serving tray or board, allowing room for the neck of the guitar to be added. Cover the sides of the guitar body with ganache to a smooth finish. Cover the top of the cake with buttercream to a smooth finish.

WHAT YOU NEED

1 quantity dark chocolate ganache (see recipe, page 21)
1 rectangular (9-by-13-inch) cake (see recipes, pages 12–13)
1 licorice twist
2 short (or 1 long) licorice sticks
7 oz dark chocolate
35 chocolate-filled vanilla sugar wafers
1 quantity buttercream (see recipe, page 20)
2 tbsp cocoa powder
food coloring: black, red & yellow
1 licorice ribbon
1 licorice sheet or licorice laces
black thread

STENCIL

Side D: Guitar Lessons

TO MAKE THE BRIDGE: Cut a 4-inch piece of licorice ribbon and press it into the buttercream below the sound hole in the guitar.

TO COMPLETE THE SOUND HOLE: Cut a 3-inch circle out of the licorice sheet, then cut a 2-inch hole in the middle of it to make a ring. Cut a piece the width of 2 sugar wafers side-by-side out of this licorice ring. Press the licorice ring into the buttercream around the sound hole, with the cut-out section of the ring pointing toward the top of the guitar, as shown. Cut a rectangular well in the cake, just wide and deep enough to fit 2 wafers side-by-side, leading from the cut-out section of the sound hole up to the edge of the top of the guitar. Using a serrated knife, cut a curve in 2 wafers to match the curve of the sound hole, then slot the curved wafers side-by-side into the well. Line up the guitar neck with these wafers and stick the end of the neck into the ganache at the top of the guitar body.

TO MAKE THE FRET MARKERS: Cut 13 strips off the licorice sheet, making them long enough to span the width of the neck. Space them evenly from the head to the sound hole, as shown.

TO MAKE THE GUITAR STRINGS: Cut 6 lengths of thread about 18 inches long each. From the remaining licorice twist, cut 6 x ½-inch pieces and 6 x ¼-inch pieces. Using ganache, stick the ½-inch pieces of licorice twist to the head of the guitar in 2 rows, trapping the end of a thread length under each. Stick the ¼-inch pieces of licorice twist to the bridge of the guitar, as shown, using ganache to glue the other end of each thread length underneath. Trim off the excess thread.

THE DO-RE-MI XYLOPHONE

INSTRUCTIONS

Bake the cake. Turn it out and leave it to cool completely.

TO MAKE THE MALLETS: Use the tip of a sharp knife to carefully "drill" a small hole in each of the candy-coated chocolate candies. Push the sharp end of a skewer into each hole, then slide a straw onto each skewer.

TO MAKE THE BARS: Roll out the red fondant to a thickness of ½ inch. Cut out a rectangle measuring 1½ inches wide by 6½ inches long. Repeat this process with every color of fondant, as shown, decreasing the length of the bar by ½ inch each time.

Make the buttercream using vegetable shortening. Place 2 tablespoons of buttercream into a piping bag and set it aside.

TO MAKE THE XYLOPHONE BASE: Level the cake and turn it over. Trace the xylophone stencil onto parchment paper and cut it out. Place your stencil in the middle of the cake and cut out 1 whole xylophone shape, then use the offcut edges of cake to cut out 2 xylophone halves. Place the xylophone halves on a serving plate and stick them together with a little buttercream. Fill the cake with buttercream, then stack the whole xylophone piece on top. Crumb coat the cake with a thin layer of buttercream, then refrigerate it until dry to the touch.

Cover the cake with buttercream to a smooth finish, then arrange the colored fondant bars on top of the cake, leaving an even space between each.

Cut a tiny portion off the tip of the piping bag that you set aside earlier. Pipe a dot of buttercream on each end of the fondant bars and place a silver dragée on each dot.

WHAT YOU NEED

1 rectangular (9-by-13-inch) cake (see recipes, pages 12–13)

2 round candy-coated chocolate candies

fondant: 6 oz red, 6 oz orange, 5½ oz yellow, 5 oz light green, 5 oz blue, 4½ oz indigo & 4 oz violet

1 quantity buttercream with a vegetable shortening base (see recipe, page 20)

14 silver dragées

cornstarch, for rolling out fondant

2 skewers

2 straws

1 piping bag

TECHNIQUES

Rolling out fondant, page 21

Leveling, page 18

Stacking & filling, page 18

Crumb coating, page 18

Creating a smooth finish, page 18

STENCIL

Side C: The Do-Re-Mi Xylophone

INSTRUCTIONS

Make the ganache and set it aside to firm up. Bake the cake. Turn it out and leave it to cool completely.

TO MAKE THE SHEET MUSIC: Melt the white chocolate or white chocolate chips, then spread a small 1¼-by-2-inch rectangle of melted chocolate on a piece of parchment paper, scraping away the messy edges with a knife. Lay the rectangle on a flat surface in the fridge to set. Once the white chocolate is dry enough to touch, melt the dark chocolate and use a toothpick dipped in melted chocolate to draw musical notes on the white chocolate rectangle. Set aside to dry.

TO MAKE THE LID AND STOOL: Trace the piano stencil onto a large piece of parchment paper, then lay the parchment paper flat on top of a baking sheet, making sure that the long, straight edge of the piano lid is on the right. Spoon the remaining melted dark chocolate into the middle of your piano stencil. Thickly spread the chocolate right to the edges with the back of a spoon. Place the tray in the fridge until the chocolate is set.

Level the cake and turn it over. Trace another piano stencil onto parchment paper and cut it out. Place your stencil on the cake, this time making sure that the long straight edge of the piano is on the left, and cut the piano shape out of the cake. For the piano stool, cut a 2-by-3-inch rectangle (or use the piano stool stencil as your guide) out of the cake offcuts. At the front of the piano, cut a 1-inch-deep well for the keyboard, as indicated on the stencil.

Cut the cake board to the shape of the piano stencil, with the long straight side on the left, and stick the cake on top with ganache. Crumb coat both the piano and the stool with a thin layer of ganache, then refrigerate the cake until dry to the touch. Cover the piano and the stool with ganache to a smooth finish.

TO MAKE THE KEYS: Using the keyboard stencil as a guide, cut the white Kit Kat bars to the correct size and place them upside down in the well, with the cut edges facing the back. Cut the licorice ribbon into 1¼-inch-long strips and arrange the strips on top of the white chocolate keys, as shown, sticking them in place with a small amount of ganache.

WHAT YOU NEED

1 quantity dark chocolate ganache (see recipe, page 21)
1 rectangular (9-by-13-inch) cake (see recipes, pages 12–13)
1 oz white chocolate or 1 tbsp white chocolate chips
18 oz dark chocolate
3 x 1½-oz packages white chocolate Kit Kat bars (12 wafers)
2 x 8-inch (approx.) licorice ribbons
3 x 7-oz Hershey's Giant milk chocolate bars (or a similar)
2 x 8-inch (approx.) solid licorice sticks
1 chocolate Pirouette cookie
toothpicks
1 rectangular (8-by-12-inch) cake board

TECHNIQUES

Melting chocolate, page 19; Leveling, page 18; Creating a smooth finish, page 18

STENCILS

Side C: Piano by Candlelight (keyboard, piano & stool)

Stack the chocolate bars in the middle of the serving plate and place the piano cake on top. Using ganache, stick 3 short pieces of solid licorice stick, approximately 1½ inches each (depending on how high your chocolate support stack is), under each corner of the piano and to the bottom of the cake board. The licorice-stick piano legs give the illusion of support while the chocolate bars hold the weight of the cake. Cut 4 short ¾-inch lengths from the remaining licorice stick and stick them to the bottom of the piano stool with ganache. Place the stool in front of the piano.

TO ATTACH THE LID: Cut the chocolate Pirouette cookie to about 2½ inches long and insert a toothpick inside it to strengthen it. Once the chocolate piano lid is completely set, remove it from the fridge, carefully peel off the parchment paper and turn the lid upside down. Using plenty of ganache, stick the long straight edge of the lid to the long straight edge of the cake, propping the front corner up with the chocolate Pirouette, as shown.

Stick the music sheet in place above the keyboard with ganache.

Notes

Keep the chocolate piano lid in the fridge until shortly before serving, as heat will weaken the structure of the chocolate, especially in warmer weather.

Once the lid is attached, keep the finished cake in a cool place until serving.

2 round (10-inch) cakes (see recipes, pages 12–13)

1 quantity buttercream (see recipe, page 20)

18 vanilla sugar wafers

9 oz white chocolate

fondant: 3½ oz each red, yellow & blue

cornstarch, for rolling out fondant

5 x 12.6-oz packages M&M's or similar candy-coated chocolate candies

1 rolling pin

A, B & C letter cookie cutters

Melting chocolate, page 19; Leveling, page 18; Stacking & filling, page 18; Crumb coating, page 18; Creating a smooth finish, page 18; Rolling out fondant, page 21

NOW I KNOW MY
ABCs

Bake the cakes. Turn them out and leave them to cool completely.

Make the buttercream and set it aside.

TO MAKE THE BLOCKS: Cut the vanilla wafers into 2½-inch squares using the tip of a serrated knife. Melt the white chocolate. Smoothly spread white chocolate on one side of each wafer square and set aside on parchment paper to dry. Once the squares are dry, you can start forming them into 3 cubes using leftover chocolate as glue to join them together. Join the first 3 sides, holding them momentarily until the chocolate hardens, then add the remaining 3 sides one at a time, again holding each one in place until the chocolate has hardened. Set cubes aside to fully dry. (If it is a hot day, or to speed up the process, you can put them in the fridge.)

Roll out the red fondant and cut it into 12 lengths measuring ¾ by 2½ inches. Cut each end of these lengths into a small point. Place the lengths along the edges of one of the cubes, making sure the strips sit evenly on each side of the joins and that the 3 fondant points meet neatly in each corner. (Use a small amount of buttercream to stick the fondant to the white chocolate if necessary.) Roll out the leftover red fondant and punch out 6 letter A's with the cookie cutter. Stick them to the middle of each cube side with a little buttercream. Repeat this process for the remaining cubes, using blue fondant for one and yellow fondant for the other, punching out a different letter for each block.

TO DECORATE THE CAKE: Level the cakes, then stack and fill them with buttercream. Crumb coat the stacked cake with a thin layer of buttercream, then refrigerate it until the cake is dry to the touch.

Cover the entire cake with buttercream to a smooth finish. Push a row of red M&M's into the buttercream around the bottom edge of the cake. Directly above the red row, add a row of yellow M&M's, slotting them into the gullies formed by the M&M's in the row below. Repeat with a layer of blue M&M's. Continue the stripy pattern all the way up the side of the cake.

Arrange the blocks on the center of the cake.

Notes

The blocks can be made up to a week in advance and stored in an airtight container.

If making more than 3 blocks, remember to allow 6 wafers per block.

WINTER
Beanie

TECHNIQUES

Leveling, page 18
Coloring, page 24
Crumb coating, page 18
Piping techniques (knit pattern), page 28

WHAT YOU NEED

1 chocolate princess cake (see recipe, page 13)
2 quantities buttercream (see recipe, page 20)
food colorings: black, blue, red & yellow
1 tbsp cocoa powder (for khaki buttercream)
1 oz fondant (any color and about the size of a golf ball)
4 piping bags
4 medium petal tips (Wilton 104)
1 palette knife
1 basket-weave tip (Wilton 47)
1 grass tip (Wilton 233)
1 skewer

INSTRUCTIONS

Bake the cake. Turn it out and leave it to cool completely. Level the cake, then place it upside down on a serving plate.

Make the buttercream and separate it into 5 equal parts. Keep 1 part uncolored, then color 1 part khaki, 1 part dark purple, and 2 parts turquoise. Feel free to choose your own color combinations.

Crumb coat the cake with a thin layer of turquoise buttercream. Refrigerate the cake until dry to the touch.

Fit a petal tip to each of the 4 piping bags and fill each with a different buttercream color.

Leave a 1¼-inch space at the top of the cake for the pom-pom. Directly below that, and using dark purple buttercream, pipe the "knit" zigzag pattern in a circle around the top of the cake. With the khaki icing, repeat the zigzag pattern directly below but slightly overlapping the dark purple row above. Pipe the third row with the uncolored buttercream and the fourth row with the turquoise frosting. Repeat the rows down the beanie, stopping 1½ inch from the bottom.

Using a palette knife, cover the remaining 1½ inch of visible cake with leftover turquoise buttercream. Change the frosting tip on the turquoise piping bag to the basket-weave tip. Using the serrated side of the tip, pipe vertical overlapping lines all around the bottom of the beanie to create a band, slightly overlapping the bottom edge of the knit pattern as you go.

TO MAKE THE POM-POM: Change the tip on the turquoise piping bag to the grass tip. Form the fondant into a ball and push a skewer into the center. Holding the skewer just underneath the ball, start at the bottom and pipe the pom-pom's long "grass" texture in ½–¾-inch strokes by piping blobs of frosting while pulling up and away from the fondant ball. Pipe clusters close together, ensuring the fondant surface is not showing through. Place the pom-pom on the beanie by carefully inserting the skewer into the top of the cake.

My 1ST Handbag

WHAT YOU NEED

1 round (8-inch) cake (see recipes, pages 12–13)
1 quantity buttercream with vegetable shortening base (see recipe, page 20)
food coloring: red
4 yellow candy necklaces
25 round pink candies
2 yellow Tootsie rolls
1 round pink Sweet Tart candy
1 piping bag
1 medium round tip (Wilton 4; optional)
1 x 16-inch-length floral wire
1 palette knife

TECHNIQUES

Leveling, page 18
Coloring, page 24
Crumb coating, page 18
Creating a smooth finish, page 18

INSTRUCTIONS

Bake the cake. Turn it out and leave it to cool completely.

Level the cake. Cut down through the top of the cake in a straight line and remove one quarter as shown. Stand the cake up on its side, with the cut edge facing downward.

Make the buttercream with a vegetable shortening base. Put two-thirds of the buttercream aside in another bowl and color the remaining third pale pink.

Crumb coat the cake with a thin layer of white buttercream and refrigerate it until dry to the touch. Place the cake on a serving plate. Cover the cake with white buttercream to a smooth finish.

TO MAKE THE HANDBAG FLAP: Gently push the edge of an 8-inch round cake pan against one side of the cake to make a round indent. Repeat on other side, then make connecting lines on the narrow sides. Using a palette knife, smoothly fill above the indent line on all sides with pale pink buttercream, as shown. (Don't worry if the edges are slightly messy, as they will be covered by a line of piping.)

Fit the round tip to the piping bag, or just cut a tiny portion off the tip of the bag, and fill the bag with pale pink buttercream. Pipe along the edges of the pink flap.

Remove the elastic from the candy necklace. Arrange candies from the candy necklace and round pink candies into flower shapes. (Each flower consists of either 1 yellow necklace center with 6 pink round candy petals, or 1 pink candy center with 5 candy necklace petals.) Press the flowers into the buttercream all over the cake.

TO MAKE THE HANDBAG CLASP: Use a small amount of white buttercream to stick on 2 yellow Tootsie rolls and then the pink Sweet Tart.

TO MAKE THE HANDLE: Thread the leftover candy necklace candies onto the floral wire, leaving enough bare wire at each end to push into the cake. Bend the wire into a U shape and insert the ends into the top of the cake. Make sure the wire is pushed deeply enough into the cake that the handle doesn't flop over.

1 quantity gingerbread (see recipe, page 14)

1 rectangular (9-by-13-inch) cake (see recipes, pages 12–13)

2 quantities royal icing (see recipe, page 20)

gel food colorings: black, blue, red & yellow

1 quantity buttercream (see recipe, page 20)

2 licorice sticks

6 piping bags

6 medium round tips (Wilton 4) or use 1 tip and wash it between colors

2 skewers

toothpicks

1 x 24-inch-length ribbon

TECHNIQUES

Coloring, page 24; Leveling, page 18; Crumb coating, page 18; Creating a smooth finish, page 18

STENCILS

Side B: The Can-We-Fix-It?Toolbox (end, side, licorice stick & individual tools)

INSTRUCTIONS

You can make the gingerbread pieces in advance and store them in an airtight container in the fridge for up to a week.

TO MAKE THE TOOLBOX AND TOOLS: Make your gingerbread dough, then roll it out on a floured surface to a thickness of 3–4 inches. Trace the toolbox stencils onto parchment paper and cut them out. Place your stencils on the dough and cut out 2 sides, 2 ends, and 1 of each tool. Remember to cut out the circle holes in the end pieces of the box and also the hole in the saw handle. Lay out all the gingerbread pieces on a baking sheet lined with baking parchment and place in the fridge or freezer for 10–15 minutes. This helps the gingerbread pieces hold their shape during baking. Bake the gingerbread, then leave it to cool completely.

Bake the cake. Turn it out and leave it to cool completely.

Make the royal icing. Color half the icing red, then evenly divide the remaining half among 5 bowls, coloring the bowls gray, green, blue, yellow, and orange. Cover the bowls with plastic wrap to prevent the icing from drying out.

TO ICE THE TOOLBOX AND TOOLS: Attach 6 medium round tips to 6 piping bags and place a couple of heaped tablespoons of each color of royal icing in a separate piping bag (or wash and dry the piping tip between colors). Using the bag of red royal icing, pipe an outline around the 2 rectangular box pieces and then spoon in more of the red royal icing, spreading the icing evenly to the outlines with a toothpick. Once the whole side is covered, gently tap the side pieces lightly on the work surface to flatten out the icing. Outline and fill all the gray portions of the tools with gray icing, then outline and fill each tool handle with a different color.

Once the base gray layer is dry to the touch, use more gray royal icing to pipe a second layer of detail on the pliers, as shown.

Make the buttercream and color it the same shade of red as the red royal icing.

TO MAKE THE INSIDE OF THE TOOLBOX: Level the cake, then turn it over. Cut 2 widths from the cake—4 by 8 inches and 3 by 8 inches. Cover the 4-inch-wide piece of cake with red buttercream, then stack the 3-inch-wide piece on top, lining up the back edge of the 2 layers to make a "step" (this will create a trough to stand the tools in). Crumb coat the cake with a thin layer of buttercream, then refrigerate it until dry to the touch.

Place the cake on a serving plate and cover it in buttercream to a smooth finish.

TO ASSEMBLE THE TOOLBOX: Once the red royal icing on the rectangle-shaped sides is dry, stick the 4 toolbox sides to the cake, using plenty of royal icing. Gently tie a ribbon around the outside of the toolbox to hold the pieces in place while the royal icing dries.

TO MAKE THE HANDLE: Check your licorice sticks against the stencil provided and cut them to size if necessary. Make an incision lengthwise down both licorice sticks without cutting all the way through, the same way you would cut open a baguette. Insert a skewer into each cut to strengthen the sticks, then join the sticks end to end by inserting a toothpick through the adjoining ends to make one long length. Insert the extended licorice stick through the holes in the toolbox as shown.

Place the dry tools in the trough, between the wall of the toolbox and the cake.

THE tea PARTY

WHAT YOU NEED

3 round (6-inch) cakes (see recipes, pages 12–13)

1 x 3-oz package yellow Jell-O

½ quantity royal icing (see recipe, page 20)

food coloring: blue

3 round shortbread cookies

5 standard ice cream cones (see page 19)

1 quantity buttercream (see recipe, page 20)

42 orange jelly beans (to make 14 flowers
  with 6 half petals each)

14 white jelly beans
  (to make 14 flower centers)

1 pastry brush

TECHNIQUES

Coloring, page 24

Leveling, page 18

Stacking & filling, page 18

Crumb coating, page 18

INSTRUCTIONS

Bake the cakes. Turn them out and leave them to cool completely.

Don't make the Jell-O until the day you are going to serve the cake. Follow the packet instructions and leave the Jell-O to cool and set in the fridge until it is the consistency of egg whites (approximately 2 hours).

Make the royal icing, then divide it into 2 bowls, leaving 1 white and coloring the other light blue. Cover the bowls with plastic wrap to prevent the icing from drying out.

TO MAKE THE TEACUPS: Place the 3 shortbread cookies on a wire rack with parchment paper underneath it, then spread light blue royal icing thickly over each cookie, letting the excess drip off the sides. Use a sharp serrated knife to cut the top "cup" off 3 of the ice cream cones and stick 1 to the wet icing of each shortbread cookie. Paint white royal icing all around the inside of the cone "cup" with a pastry brush. Set the cups aside to dry. To make the teacup handles, cut out a cross section from the narrow end of each of the 3 offcut cones. Trim each of the cross-section pieces to make a handle shape and stick one to the side of each cup with royal icing.

TO MAKE THE TEAPOT: Make the buttercream and color it light blue to match the royal icing. Level 2 of the cakes. Stack and fill the cakes with buttercream, then place the third domed cake on top of the stack. To make the teapot shape, use a serrated knife to carve the bottom edge of the cake stack so it is rounded underneath, then carve off the top edge of the cake to enhance the natural dome of the cake, giving it more of a sphere shape.

Crumb coat the cake with a thin layer of blue buttercream, then refrigerate the cake until dry to the touch. Place the cake on a serving plate, then thickly cover the cake in blue buttercream to a smooth finish.

TO MAKE THE TEAPOT LID: Use a sharp serrated knife to cut the top ¾ inch off the open end of an ice cream cone, just under the bowl shape. Set aside the rest of the cone to use as a spout. Place the lid on top of the cake and fill it with buttercream.

TO MAKE THE SPOUT: Cut the open end of the reserved cone on a diagonal to make an angled spout. Cut the tip off the narrow end of the cone to shape the lip of the spout. Place the spout in position on the teapot, pressing it into the buttercream.

TO MAKE THE TEAPOT HANDLE: Cut the top ¾ inch off the open end of the remaining cone. Cut this piece into 2 semicircles and push the pieces into the buttercream so the 2 ends just touch, making it look as if the handle is 1 piece. From the cone offcut, cut a cross section ½-inch wide and place it on top of the teapot lid as a handle.

TO DECORATE THE TEAPOT: Cut all the jelly beans in half crosswise and arrange 6 orange halves around 1 white half to make a flower pattern. Press these flowers into the buttercream, spacing them randomly all over the teapot, as shown.

Once the royal icing inside the teacups is dry to the touch and the Jell-O is the consistency of egg whites, spoon the Jell-O into the teacups. Refrigerate the finished cake until serving.

INSTRUCTIONS

Bake the cakes. Turn them out and leave them to cool completely.

Make the buttercream. Divide it evenly among 5 bowls and color the bowls blue, yellow, pink, light green, and orange, trying to match the colors of the M&M's that will be used to fill the cake.

Level the cakes. Cut each cake in half horizontally to make 4 layers. Take 3 layers of cake and stack them together. Place the can cutter in the center of the stacked cake and push it down all the way through the layers to punch out the middle. Discard the cake center. Leave the other cake layer whole.

TO STACK THE CAKES: Spread a little of the blue buttercream on one of the uncut layers of cake and place it buttercream side down on the serving plate. Place the can as a marker in the center of this layer and spread yellow buttercream around it. Remove the can and stack one of the ring-shaped layers on top of the yellow buttercream layer and spread it with pink buttercream. Stack the other ring-shaped layer on the pink buttercream layer and spread it with light green buttercream. Pour the M&M's into the central hole and stack the last uncut layer of cake on top.

TO PIPE THE RUFFLES: Fit each piping bag with a petal tip and fill the bags with the individual colors (if you are using one tip, wash and dry it as needed). Take the piping bag with the blue buttercream and hold it so that the tip is perpendicular to the cake, with the wider side of the tip touching the cake and the narrow side facing outward. Steadily squeeze a line of frosting around the base of the cake in an up-and-down zigzag motion to create a ruffled effect that is about ½ inch high, going halfway up the first layer of cake. (Practice the ruffle frosting on the counter before you start on the cake—it is much easier than it looks!) Repeat the next layer of blue ruffles directly above the first so that the bottom layer of cake is completely covered. It is best to start and finish each row of frosting at the same point so the joins will all be at the back of the cake.

Repeat this process with the yellow, pink, and light green frosting, creating 2 rows of ruffles for each color, as shown, until the whole side of the cake is covered.

Cover the top of the cake with a thin layer of orange buttercream, then pipe the top as follows: Start in the center with the wide opening of the petal tip facing down toward the cake and the thin opening facing up. Pipe a small wiggly circle in the middle of the cake, then repeat, piping ruffle circles all the way out to the edge of the cake, with the last circle overlapping the green edge, as shown.

Piñata SURPRISE!

WHAT YOU NEED

2 round (8-inch) vanilla cakes (see recipe, page 12)

2 quantities buttercream (see recipe, page 20)

food coloring: blue, red & yellow

8 oz (1⅓ cups) M&M's or similar candy-coated chocolate candies

5 piping bags

5 medium petal tips (Wilton 104) or use 1 tip and wash it between colors

1 can cutter (see page 17)

TECHNIQUES

Coloring, page 24

Leveling, page 18

Stacking & filling, page 18

The EMOTICONS

2 quantities royal icing (see recipe, page 20)
6 round (6-inch) cakes (see recipes, pages 12–13)
2 quantities buttercream (see recipe, page 20)
gel food colorings: black, blue, red & yellow
5 piping bags
5 medium round tips (Wilton 4)

STENCILS

Side C: The Emoticons

TECHNIQUES

Royal icing (flood consistency), page 20
Coloring, page 24
Leveling, page 18
Crumb coating, page 18
Creating a smooth finish, page 18

INSTRUCTIONS

Make the royal icing faces at least a day in advance to allow for drying time.

TO MAKE THE ROYAL ICING FACES: Trace the stencils onto parchment paper and place them on a baking sheet. Make the royal icing. Place 7 oz royal icing in 1 bowl and color it bright yellow. Place 1 oz each of royal icing in 5 bowls. Keep 1 bowl white and color the rest black, red, pink, and light blue. Remember the colors will intensify as the royal icing dries.

Fit a medium round tip to each piping bag and place a large tablespoonful of each color into a separate bag. Cover the bowls of remaining icing with plastic wrap to prevent the icing from drying out. Pipe the outlines of each emoticon directly onto the parchment paper stencils, using the colors as shown. Set the tray of piped emoticons aside to dry.

Once the piped outlines are dry to the touch, slowly add water to each bowl of leftover royal icing so that the icing becomes flood consistency. Flood the icing inside each piped outline with the matching color and leave the emoticons to dry overnight in a dry environment.

Bake the cakes, turn them out, and leave them to cool completely.

Make the buttercream and color it bright yellow to match the yellow royal icing.

Level the cakes, then crumb coat them with a thin layer of buttercream. Refrigerate the cakes until dry to the touch. Place the cakes on serving plates and cover them with buttercream to a smooth finish.

Once completely dry, carefully peel the emoticons off the parchment paper and place one on each of the cakes.

The
"IT'S MY
PARTY!"
CAKE

WHAT YOU NEED

3 round (8-inch) cakes (see recipes, pages 12–13)
1 quantity buttercream (see recipe, page 20)
fondant: 9 oz white
2 cups (14 oz approx.) sprinkles
cornstarch, for rolling out fondant
1 round (8-inch) cake board
2 paper towels
1 paintbrush

TECHNIQUES

Leveling, page 18
Stacking & filling, page 18
Creating a smooth finish, page 18
Fondant bow, page 23

INSTRUCTIONS

Bake the cakes. Turn them out and leave them to cool completely.

Make the buttercream.

Level the cakes. Stack and fill the cakes, then secure the stacked cake to the cake board with a little buttercream (this will hold the cake when you add the sprinkles). Cover the cake with buttercream to a smooth finish.

TO DECORATE THE CAKE WITH SPRINKLES: Place a bowl upside down in the middle of a shallow baking pan then sit the cake on top. Have fun with this part, because it gets messy! Pour sprinkles over the top of the cake and gently press them into the buttercream with your fingers, using the paintbrush to brush the excess sprinkles into the baking dish below. To decorate the sides of the cake, take small handfuls of sprinkles and run your hand down the side of the cake, pressing the sprinkles in and letting the excess fall into the baking dish. Repeat this process all the way around the cake, filling in any gaps. Place the cake on a serving plate.

TO MAKE THE BOW: Refer to page 23 for instructions. Keep the paper towel supports in place.

TO MAKE THE RIBBON TAILS: Roll out white fondant to a thickness of ⅛–¼ inch and cut out 2 rectangles measuring 3 by 8 inches. Cut off 1 end of the rectangle diagonally and pinch widthwise at the other end. Repeat this process with the other rectangle. Place the pinched ends together in the center of the cake, leaving the diagonally cut ends to drape down the side of the cake. Gently place the bow loops (with their paper-towel supports still in place) upright on top of the tail pieces.

Once the bow loops are dry enough to hold their shape, remove the paper towels.

Note
Use real ribbon instead of a fondant bow if you prefer.

the BIRTHDAY cake

TECHNIQUES

Rolling out fondant, page 21
Leveling, page 18
Stacking & filling, page 18
Creating a smooth finish, page 18
Covering a cake with fondant, page 23
Supporting a stack, page 19

WHAT YOU NEED

fondant: 52 oz white (3 lb to cover cake and 1¾ oz to decorate candles), 18 oz yellow, 3½ oz orange, 1¾ oz blue, 1¾ oz white, 1¾ oz purple, 1¾ oz pale pink, 1¾ oz green & 1¾ oz red
cornstarch, for rolling out fondant
2 round (8-inch) cakes (see recipes, pages 12–13)
2 round (6-inch) cakes (see recipes, pages 12–13)
2 quantities buttercream or ganache (see recipes, pages 20–21)
1 round (6-inch) cake board
5 skewers or dowels
1 rolling pin

INSTRUCTIONS

Make the candles at least a day in advance to allow for drying time.

TO MAKE THE CANDLES: Trace the candle stencil onto parchment paper and cut it out. Every candle has 3 layers: a yellow fondant backing, a colored fondant candle-stem layer on top, then assorted shapes on top of the second layer for decoration. Roll out yellow fondant, place the stencil on top of the fondant, and cut out 20 candles. Lay the fondant candles on a baking sheet lined with parchment paper.

Trace the flame-center stencil onto paper and cut it out. Roll out the orange fondant and cut out 20 flame centers using this stencil. Stick the orange centers to the yellow flames with a small amount of water.

Roll out fondant in assorted colors, including the leftover yellow and orange fondant. Using the stencil, cut out 20 candle stems. Stick the colored stems to the yellow candles, on the same side as the orange flames, with a little water. Roll out the remaining colored fondant and cut out assorted shapes to decorate the face of each candle as desired. Stick on these shapes with a small amount of water. Leave to dry in a warm, dry spot overnight.

Bake the cakes. Turn them out and leave them to cool completely. Make the buttercream or ganache. Level the cakes. Stack and fill the 8-inch cakes with buttercream or ganache. Cover the cake stack in buttercream or ganache to a smooth finish. Place the 8-inch stacked cakes on a serving plate and set them aside.

Stack and fill the 6-inch cakes with buttercream or ganache. Stick the 6-inch cake stack to the 6-inch cake board, using a small amount of buttercream or ganache. Cover the cake stack in buttercream or ganache to a smooth finish. Set aside.

Roll out 1¾ lb white fondant to a thickness of ¼ inch and a diameter of 16 inches. Place fondant over the 8-inch cake and smooth and trim it.

Repeat this process again for the 6-inch cake, this time rolling out 21 oz white fondant to a thickness of ¼ inch and a diameter of 14 inches.

Support and stack the cakes, using the skewers or dowels.

Hold the candles against the cake and cut them to varying lengths. Using a little buttercream, stick 10 fondant candles to the bottom tier of the cake, spacing them evenly around it. Repeat this process for the top tier of the cake, placing the 10 remaining candles on the top tier in the gaps between the lower candles.

Note

The variety of colors and shapes on the candles is limited only by your imagination. Have fun!

1 quantity dark chocolate ganache (see recipe, page 21)
2 round (8-inch) cakes (see recipes, pages 12–13)
1 quantity buttercream (see recipe, page 20)
food colorings: blue, green, red & yellow
2 x 6.8-oz Hershey's Special Dark Mildly Sweet
    Chocolate Bar (or a similar large dark chocolate bar)
5 piping bags
1 palette knife or icing smoother

Leveling, page 18
Stacking & filling, page 18
Coloring, page 24
Melting chocolate, page 19

The
CHOCOLATE
Rainbow
WATERFALL

INSTRUCTIONS

Make the ganache and set it aside to firm up.

Bake the cakes. Turn them out and leave them to cool completely.

Level the cakes. Stack and fill the cakes with ganache. Place the stacked cake on a serving plate.

Make the buttercream. Divide it evenly among 5 different bowls. Color 1 pink, 1 orange, 1 yellow, 1 light green, and 1 light blue. Place each color in a separate piping bag and cut the tip off each to create an opening ¾ inch in diameter.

Starting at the bottom of the cake, pipe a thick line of light blue buttercream around the base. Repeat with light green buttercream, then yellow, orange, and pink. (Don't be concerned about getting the top line perfect as it will be covered with ganache later.)

Holding a palette knife or an icing smoother vertically, in one smooth motion wipe around the cake, removing any excess frosting. This will blend the colors together. Be sure to wipe your palette knife or icing smoother clean each time you remove the excess frosting.

TO PREPARE THE CHOCOLATE BAR: First you need to make a dagger-shaped extension in one corner of the chocolate bar. This will support the chocolate bar and stop it from falling over. Roughly chop half of one of the dark chocolate bars and melt it in a bowl set over a pan of simmering water, or in the microwave. Unwrap the second bar of chocolate and place it on a sheet of parchment paper on a flat surface. Pour the melted chocolate over one of the corners of the chocolate bar and then diagonally down, directly onto the parchment paper, to create a dagger shape about 3 inches long and 1½ inches wide. Set the chocolate aside on a flat surface to cool and harden. (On a very hot day, you might need to put it on a tray in the fridge to cool.)

Before assembling the cake, check that the ganache is at a spreadable consistency, heating it slightly if too stiff. Spread the ganache over the top of the cake, carefully pushing it to the edges to allow the ganache to drip over the sides of the cake but not form a pool at its base.

With a knife, make a cut in the middle of the cake at least 3 inches deep. Insert the chocolate dagger into the cut so that the chocolate bar appears to be standing up on its corner. Spoon extra ganache around the base of the chocolate bar to make it look like it is melting. Taking a bite out of the top corner is optional!

Note
If using a milk chocolate bar instead of a dark chocolate bar, remember to make milk chocolate ganache to match.

The "I ♥ U" Cake

TECHNIQUES

Coloring, page 24
Leveling, page 18
Crumb coating, page 18
Creating a smooth finish, page 18
Rolling out fondant, page 21

WHAT YOU NEED

1 quantity dark chocolate ganache (see recipe, page 21)
1 quantity royal icing (see recipe, page 20)
gel food coloring: red
1 rectangular (9-by-13-inch) cake (see recipes, pages 12–13)
fondant: 25 oz red
1 box chocolates, assorted shapes
cornstarch, for rolling out fondant
mini cupcake liners
2 piping bags
2 small round tips (Wilton 3; optional)
1 small rolling pin

STENCIL

Side D: The "I ♥ U" Cake

INSTRUCTIONS

Make the dark chocolate ganache and set it aside to firm up.

TO DECORATE THE CHOCOLATES: Make the royal icing and divide it between 2 bowls. Keep one bowl of icing white and color the second bowl red. Set up 2 piping bags, fitting a small round tip to each (or just cut a tiny portion off the tip of each bag). Fill one bag with white royal icing and the other with red royal icing. Pipe various designs on the chocolates, as shown, and set them aside to dry.

Bake the cake. Turn it out and leave it to cool completely. Level the cake and turn it over. Trace the heart stencil onto parchment paper and cut it out. Place your stencil on the cake and cut out the shape. Crumb coat the cake with a thin layer of ganache. Refrigerate the cake until dry to the touch.

Place the cake on a serving plate and cover it with ganache to a smooth finish.

Roll out red fondant to a thickness of ¼ inch. Cut a rectangular strip about 30 inches long by ¼ inch wide. Carefully roll the fondant up around a small rolling pin dusted with cornstarch so you can lift it to the cake without tearing or stretching its shape. Holding the rolling pin vertically and starting inside the V at the top of the heart, unroll the fondant around the edge of the cake, gently sticking the fondant to the ganache-covered sides as you go. Trim the excess fondant where the ends meet. The fondant lip will stick up above the sides of the cake, creating a box for the chocolates to sit in.

Place each chocolate in a mini cupcake liner and arrange the chocolates on the cake.

the NAKED CAKE

WHAT YOU NEED

2 round (6-inch) cakes (see recipes, pages 12–13)

1 quantity sugar syrup (see recipe, page 15)

1 cup superfine sugar

1⅓ cups mixed berries

1 quantity buttercream (see recipe, page 20)

1 pastry brush

1 palette knife or icing smoother

TECHNIQUES

Leveling, page 18

Stacking & filling, page 18

Creating a smooth finish, page 18

INSTRUCTIONS

Bake the cakes. Turn them out and leave them to cool completely.

Make the sugar syrup and allow it to cool.

TO MAKE THE SUGARED BERRIES: First, tip the superfine sugar onto a large plate. Using a pastry brush, lightly cover each berry with the cooled sugar syrup then roll it in superfine sugar. Place the berries on a piece of parchment paper to dry.

Make the buttercream. Level the cakes, then cut both cakes in half horizontally to create 4 layers. Place the bottom layer of cake on a serving plate, then stack and fill the cakes with buttercream, using a generous amount of buttercream between each layer. Cover the cake with buttercream to a smooth finish on top.

Using a palette knife or cake scraper, scrape off the buttercream around the sides of the cake so it is barely covered and the cake underneath shows through.

Arrange the sugared berries on top of the cake just before serving.

Notes

Make the sugared berries on the same day you serve the cake.

Lightly beaten egg whites can be used in place of sugar syrup if desired.

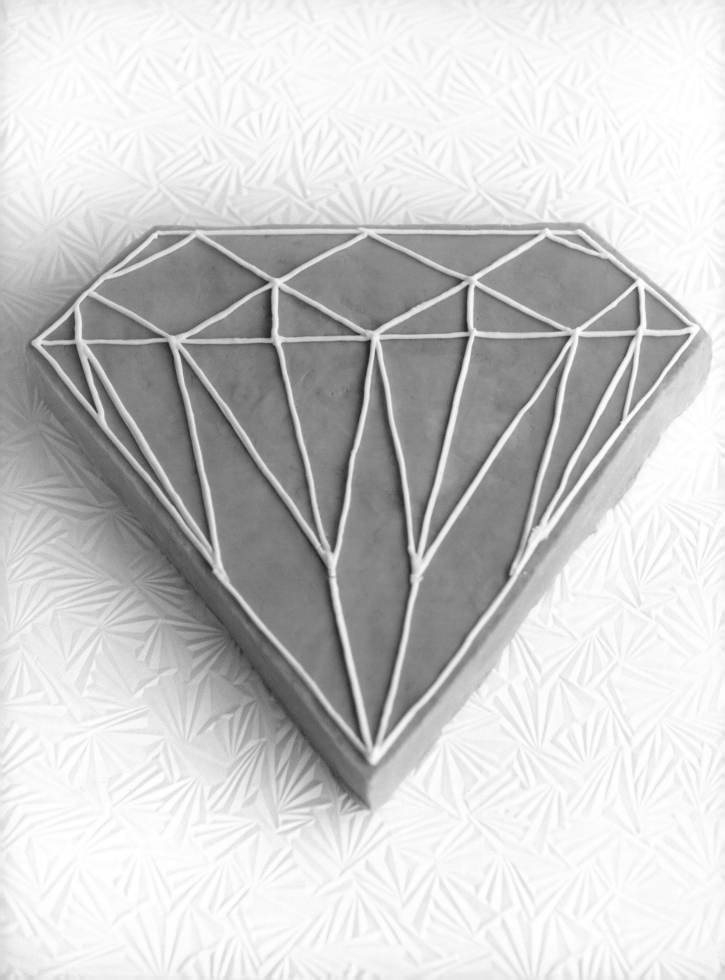

A Girl's BEST friend

WHAT YOU NEED

2 rectangular (9-by-13-inch) cakes
   (see recipes, pages 12–13)
2 quantities buttercream (see recipe, page 20)
food colorings: blue & yellow
1 piping bag
1 large round tip (Wilton 6)
1 packet toothpicks
1 ruler

TECHNIQUES

Coloring, page 24
Leveling, page 18
Crumb coating, page 18
Creating a smooth finish, page 18

STENCIL

Side D: A Girl's Best Friend

INSTRUCTIONS

Bake the cakes. Turn them out and leave them to cool completely.

Make the buttercream. Fit the large round tip to the piping bag, fill the bag with 3 heaped tablespoons of buttercream, then set the bag aside. Color the remaining buttercream mint green.

Level the cakes and turn them over.

Trace the half-diamond stencil onto parchment paper and cut it out. Place your stencil on one cake and cut out the half-diamond shape. Turn the stencil over, place it on the second cake and cut the other half-diamond out. Arrange the two cakes into a diamond shape on your serving plate and stick the halves together with mint-green buttercream.

Crumb coat the cake with a thin layer of mint green buttercream and refrigerate it until dry to the touch, then cover the cake with mint green buttercream to a smooth finish.

TO MAKE THE DIAMOND FACETS: Carefully place your stencil over the cake and mark out the points of the diamond by poking toothpicks through the parchment paper and into the cake. Remove the stencil, leaving the toothpicks sticking out of the cake as a guide. Turn the stencil over and repeat. Using a ruler, indent straight lines in the buttercream, between the toothpicks (the indents will be your guide for piping the white lines). Remove the toothpicks and pipe over the indented lines with the white buttercream to create the diamond's outline.

The PAINTER'S palette

WHAT YOU NEED

3 round (8-inch) cakes (see recipes, pages 12–13)
1 quantity buttercream or ganache (see recipes, pages 20–21)
fondant: 3 lb white
3 tbsp vodka
gel food colorings: blue & red
cornstarch, for rolling out fondant
3 new food-safe sponges
1 rolling pin

TECHNIQUES

Leveling, page 18
Crumb coating, page 18
Stacking & filling, page 18
Creating a smooth finish, page 18
Covering a cake with fondant, page 23

INSTRUCTIONS

Bake the cakes. Turn them out and leave them to cool completely.

Make the buttercream or ganache and set it aside to firm up.

Level the cakes, then stack and fill them with buttercream or ganache. Place the stacked cake on a serving plate. Cover the cake with buttercream or ganache to a smooth finish.

Roll out white fondant to a thickness of ¼ inch and a diameter of 20 inches. Place the fondant over the cake, then smooth and trim it.

TO PAINT THE CAKE: Put 1 tablespoon of vodka in each of 3 small bowls. Add a small amount of blue coloring to one bowl, add a small amount of red coloring to the second bowl, and combine both blue and red colorings in the last bowl to make purple. Using a separate sponge for each color, dip a sponge in the vodka color mixture, then wipe the sponge onto the fondant to create a random, blended pattern. Because vodka evaporates quickly, the colors won't take long to dry.

Note

If you don't mix the vodka and gel color together completely, there will be different shades of blue, pink, and purple on your sponge in every stroke! Dip the sponge in the gel areas of the mixture for more concentrated colors and in the weakly colored vodka areas for a paler color.

THE Flowerpot

TECHNIQUES

Coloring, page 24
Piping techniques (flowers & leaves), page 31
Leveling, page 18
Stacking & filling, page 18
Crumb coating, page 18
Creating a smooth finish, page 18

WHAT YOU NEED

1 quantity royal icing (see recipe, page 20)
gel food colorings: blue, green, red, yellow & black
½ quantity dark chocolate ganache (see recipe, page 21)
3 round (6-inch) chocolate cakes (see recipe, page 13)
1 quantity buttercream (see recipe, page 20)
4 piping bags
3 small petal tips (Wilton 102) or use 1 tip and wash it between colors
1 small round tip (Wilton 3)
1 leaf tip (Wilton 352)
1 icing smoother

INSTRUCTIONS

Make the flowers and leaves at least a day in advance to allow for drying time.

TO MAKE THE FLOWERS AND LEAVES: Make the royal icing and divide it evenly among 5 bowls. Color the bowls yellow, light green, dark green, light purple, and dark purple. Fit the petal tips to 3 separate piping bags. Fill 1 with yellow, 1 with light purple, and 1 with dark purple royal icing. Pipe the flowers and leaves directly onto parchment paper placed on a flat surface. Make approximately 20 flowers, varying the color combinations and sizes, and approximately 60 leaves. Leave the royal icing leaves and flowers out overnight to harden in a dry environment.

Make the ganache and set it aside to firm up.

Bake the cakes. Turn them out and leave them to cool completely.

Make the buttercream and color it terra-cotta.

Level the cakes, being careful to keep one of the offcut domes intact. Set this dome aside. Crumble the rest of the cake offcuts and set them aside to use as chocolate soil later. Stack and fill the cakes with ganache. Cut a 4-inch circle out of parchment paper and place it on top of the cake in the center of the cake stack.

To form the slanted edges of the flowerpot, use a serrated knife to cut a straight line from the edge of the 4-inch circle at the top of the cake to the bottom outer edge of the full 6-inch circle at the bottom. Crumb coat the stacked cake with a thin layer of buttercream, then refrigerate it until dry to the touch

TO FROST THE FLOWERPOT: Thickly cover the sides of the cake with buttercream to a smooth finish. Hold your icing smoother at the same angle as the sides of the flowerpot and press it into the thick buttercream 1½ inches from the base of the cake, scraping away excess frosting to form a rim at the base. Refrigerate the cake for 15–30 minutes so that the buttercream can firm up, then carefully flip the pot over and place it upright on the serving plate.

Spread ganache on top of the flowerpot and place the reserved dome offcut on top. Cover the dome with ganache and press the crumbled cake soil on top. Peel the flowers and leaves off the parchment paper. Arrange 3 leaves under every flower, all over the dome of the cake, sticking them in place with ganache.

fondant: 1¾ lb white & 10½ oz mixture of white, light blue, light purple & pale pink

2 round (6-inch) cakes (see recipes, pages 12–13)

2 round (8-inch) cakes (see recipes, pages 12–13)

2 quantities buttercream (see recipe, page 20)

food colorings: blue & red

cornstarch, for rolling out fondant

3 hydrangea cutters in different sizes (see page 17)

1 round (6-inch) cake board

5 dowels or skewers

1 rolling pin

Rolling out fondant, page 21

Leveling, page 18

Stacking & filling, page 18

Creating a smooth finish, page 18

Covering a cake with fondant, page 23

Supporting a stack, page 19

HEAVENLY
Hydrangea

INSTRUCTIONS

Make the hydrangea petals at least a day in advance to allow for drying time.

TO MAKE THE HYDRANGEA PETALS: Lay a sheet of plastic wrap over an uneven surface (such as an empty egg carton or some cutlery). Take approximately 1½ oz of each of the white, light purple, pale pink, and light blue fondants and knead them together slightly to create a marbled effect. Roll out the fondant. Dip the hydrangea cutters in cornstarch, then press out various-sized flowers. Lay the flowers over the plastic wrap to dry. The uneven surface will cause them to dry in unique 3-D shapes, which will give the cake more depth. Repeat the process again, adding more assorted fondant colors each time for different marbled effects. Continue until 10½ oz of fondant has been formed into flowers.

Bake the cakes. Turn them out and cool them completely.

Make the buttercream and color it light purple.

Level the cakes. Place one of the 8-inch cakes on a serving plate. Stack and fill the 8-inch cakes with buttercream. Cover the cake in buttercream to a smooth finish, then refrigerate until dry to the touch.

Roll out 1¾ lb white fondant into a circle that is approximately 16 inches in diameter and ¼ inch thick. Place the rolled-out fondant over the 8-inch cake, then smooth and trim it.

Stack and fill the 6-inch cakes. Stick the bottom of this cake stack to the cake board with a small amount of buttercream. Cover the cake in buttercream to a smooth finish. Support and stack the cakes using the dowels or skewers.

Press your fondant hydrangeas onto the buttercream on the top tier, ensuring the various colors are scattered randomly. Start by dotting bigger flowers all over the cake, then fill in the gaps.

You can use more buttercream to stick the flowers on if necessary.

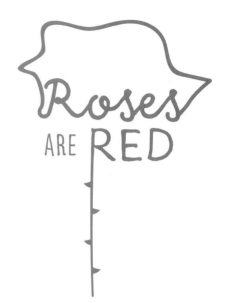

INSTRUCTIONS

Make the white chocolate ganache and set it aside to firm up.

Make the sugar syrup and allow it to cool.

Bake the cakes. Turn them out and leave them to cool completely.

TO MAKE THE SUGARED ROSES: Remove the leaves and thorns from the rose stems and discard them. Tip superfine sugar onto a plate. Using a pastry brush, lightly paint the petals with the cooled sugar syrup, and then sprinkle each with superfine sugar, completing one rose at a time. Place the flowers in a vase to dry (the stems can still be in water to keep the roses fresh).

Level the cakes, then stack and fill them with ganache. Crumb coat the stacked cake with a thin layer of ganache, then refrigerate it until dry to the touch.

Place the cake on a serving plate and completely cover it in ganache. Use a palette knife to create a textured look.

Push the flower picks into the top of the cake, making sure that they're evenly spaced. Shortly before serving the cake, trim the rose stems to your desired length and insert them into the flower picks.

Notes

The purpose of the flower picks is to prevent the flower stems from seeping sap into the cake. They are available from specialty cake stores, but if you cannot source them you can use wider smoothie straws as a substitute. Just make sure you wrap the ends of the stems with plastic wrap before inserting them into the straws.

Sugared roses will continue to open, so choose flowers that are semiclosed and will last well without water once they're inserted into the cake.

You can use lightly beaten egg whites instead of sugar syrup if you wish.

WHAT YOU NEED

1 quantity white chocolate ganache (see recipe, page 21)
1 quantity sugar syrup (see recipe, page 15)
3 round (6-inch) cakes (see recipes, pages 12–13)
15 fresh roses
1 cup superfine sugar
1 pastry brush
15 flower picks (see page 17); see note at left
1 palette knife

TECHNIQUES

Leveling, page 18
Stacking & filling, page 18
Crumb coating, page 18

STENCIL

Side B: The Take-a-Bow Cake

WHAT YOU NEED

1 rectangular (9-by-13-inch) cake (see recipes, pages 12–13)

1 quantity buttercream or ganache (see recipes, pages 20–21)

fondant: 9 oz red, 9 oz black & 1¾ lb white

cornstarch, for rolling out fondant

3–4 silicone mats, for rolling out and covering fondant

paper towels

1 rolling pin

TECHNIQUES

Leveling, page 18

Stacking & filling, page 18

Creating a smooth finish, page 18

Rolling out fondant, page 21

Covering a cake with fondant, page 23

Fondant bow, page 23

INSTRUCTIONS

Bake the cake. Turn it out and leave it to cool completely.

Level the cake. Measure and cut 2-by-6-inch squares out of the cake. Make the buttercream or ganache. Stack and fill the cakes, then place the stacked cake on a serving plate and cover it with buttercream or ganache to a smooth finish. Try to keep your edges sharp, as this will give your finished product a better box look.

TO MAKE THE GIFT WRAP: Prepare a silicone mat by lightly dusting it with cornstarch, then thinly roll out the white fondant to a thickness of ⅛ inch. Cut out a rectangle measuring 14 by 6 inches. Lift the fondant rectangle gently to check that it is not sticking to the mat, then cut it lengthwise into ½-inch-wide strips. Cover the fondant with another silicone mat or a damp kitchen towel to prevent it from drying out. Repeat this process with the black fondant.

Prepare another silicone mat by lightly dusting it with cornstarch, then thinly roll out the remaining white fondant to a thickness of ⅛ inch and cut out a 12-by-14-inch rectangle. This is the base for your stripes. Brush the fondant with a small amount of water to make it slightly damp so that the stripes will stick to it. Lay the black and white fondant lengths on the white base, alternating the colors to make a striped pattern. Lightly roll over the top of the stripy pattern with your rolling pin to bind the stripes together. Place a silicone mat on top and turn the mats and striped fondant upside down.

Trace the stencil onto parchment paper and cut it out. Carefully peel off the top silicone mat. Place your stencil on the white side of your striped fondant and cut out the shape. Lift the silicone mat, with the fondant on top of it, and turn it upside down over the cake. Carefully peel off the silicone mat, then smooth the top of the cake and fold the sides down. Last, fold the pointed flaps around the side of the cake, as shown, just as if you are wrapping the edges of a real present.

TO MAKE THE RIBBON: Roll out the red fondant to a thickness of ¼ inch, then cut out 2 lengths measuring 1½ by 14 inches. Lay each length over the center of the cake to make a cross, trimming the excess and tucking the ends underneath the cake.

TO MAKE THE BOW: Refer to page 23 for instructions. Keep the paper towel supports in place.

TO MAKE THE RIBBON TAILS: Roll out the red fondant to ⅛ inch thick and cut out 2 rectangles measuring 1½ by 5 inches. Cut a V out of one end of the rectangle and pinch it widthwise at the other end. Repeat this process with the second rectangle. Place the pinched ends together in the center of the cake and arrange the diagonally cut ends so that they drape over the cake and down the sides. Gently place the bow loops (with their paper-towel supports still in place) upright on top of the tail pieces.

Once the bow loops are dry enough to hold their shape, remove the paper towels.

Notes

Use real ribbon instead of a fondant bow if desired.

If you prefer, make the gift wrap with one color of fondant.

IT'S
MARBELOUS!

3 round (8-inch) cakes (see recipes, pages 12–13)
1 quantity buttercream or ganache (see recipes, pages 20–21)
fondant: 9 oz black, 26 oz white & 14 oz gray
cornstarch, for rolling out fondant
1 rolling pin

TECHNIQUES

Leveling, page 18
Stacking & filling, page 18
Creating a smooth finish, page 18
Rolling out fondant, page 21
Covering a cake with fondant, page 23

INSTRUCTIONS

Bake the cakes. Turn them out and leave them to cool completely. Make the buttercream or ganache.

Level the cakes, then stack and fill them with buttercream or ganache. Place the stacked cake on a serving plate and cover it with buttercream or ganache to a smooth finish.

TO CREATE A MARBLED EFFECT: On a surface lightly dusted with cornstartch, use your hands to separately roll the black, white, and gray fondant into ropes about 12 inches long (they will be different thicknesses). Stack and press the ropes together to make one thick rope.

Twist the rope, rolling it to create a spiral pattern. The more you twist, the more marbled your pattern will become. Fold this twisted length in half and gently press it together without mixing the colors anymore. If you want thicker stripes or a block marble pattern, roll out the fondant at this point. Otherwise, repeat this process, pressing your fondant together into one thick rope, twisting it into a spiral pattern, and then folding it in half.

Roll out the fondant to a thickness of ¼ inch and a diameter of 16 inches. Remember to check both sides of the fondant before laying it over your cake because each side is unique. Choose your favorite!

Place the fondant over the cake and smooth and trim it.

Notes
The colors within the marbling effect can be as mixed or as separate as you wish. The more times you repeat the roll, twist, and fold process, the more mixed the marble pattern will become.

The thinner you roll the fondant, the more marbled it will look because the darker colors show through the white fondant.

Have fun and play around with the quantities and colors of fondant you marble. Remember, dark colors show through the most, so don't overdo them!

THE MESSY cake

TECHNIQUES

Melting chocolate, page 19
Leveling, page 18
Stacking & filling, page 18
Supporting a stack, page 19

WHAT YOU NEED

2 round (6-inch) cakes (see recipes, pages 12–13)
2 round (8-inch) cakes (see recipes, pages 12–13)
10 (approx.) lollipops: green, pink & yellow
20 hard raspberry candies or other hard red candies
7 oz white chocolate
2 quantities buttercream (see recipe, page 20)
silver dragées
10 nasturtium flowers or any edible flowers (pesticide-free)
20 Sixlets or edible chocolate pearls
2 large zippered plastic bags
5 skewers
1 round (6-inch) cake board
1 rolling pin
1 palette knife

INSTRUCTIONS

Bake the cakes. Turn them out and leave them to cool completely.

TO MAKE THE MULTICOLORED CANDY SHARDS: Preheat the oven to 320°F and line a baking sheet with parchment paper. Place the lollipops in a zippered plastic bag, cover the bag with a kitchen towel, and hit the bag with a rolling pin until the lollipops are in large pieces. Discard the lollipop sticks, put the large pieces of lollipop on the parchment paper in a random fashion, and put the baking sheet in the oven for around 5 minutes until the lollipops melt together into one flat multicolored sheet. Watch closely to make sure the sugar doesn't burn. Repeat this process with 5 of the raspberry candies on a separate sheet. Set the baking sheets of melted candies aside to cool, taking care, as melted sugar is extremely hot.

TO MAKE THE WHITE CHOCOLATE SHARDS: Smash the remaining raspberry candies, as above. Line a baking sheet with parchment paper. Melt the white chocolate and spread it over the parchment paper so that it is ⅛ inch thick. Sprinkle the broken pieces of raspberry candies, along with silver dragées, over the melted chocolate and set this aside to harden.

Make the buttercream and level the cakes. Stack and fill the 8-inch cakes. Place the 8-inch cake stack on a serving plate. Stack and fill the 6-inch cakes. Stick the bottom of the 6-inch cake stack to the cake board using a small amount of buttercream. Support and stack the cakes.

Thickly spread buttercream all over the cakes using a palette knife to give the cake natural-looking swirls and texture.

Break the melted candies into small shards and the melted chocolate into larger shards. Randomly arrange the shards, flowers, Sixlets, and raspberry candies or red hard candies all over the cake, pressing them into the buttercream as you go. Have fun!

MERINGUE FRENZY

WHAT YOU NEED

1 quantity meringue kisses (see recipe, page 15)
½ cup finely chopped hazelnuts
cocoa powder, for dusting the kisses
2 tbsp freeze-dried coffee
1 quantity dark chocolate ganache (see recipe, page 21)
3 round (8-inch) cakes (see recipes, pages 12–13)
3 baking sheets
1 piping bag
1 extra-large round tip (Wilton 1A)

INSTRUCTIONS

Make the meringue kisses at least a day in advance of serving the cake.

Make the meringue mixture.

TO PIPE THE MERINGUE KISSES: Fit the extra-large round tip to the piping bag, fill it with one-third of the meringue mixture, and pipe small kisses with a 1¼-inch base onto one baking sheet, keeping them as uniform in size and shape as possible. To make a kiss shape, squeeze the bag until the circle is the size of the base you want, then release the pressure and pull up to create a peak on the kiss. Sprinkle this first baking sheet of meringue kisses with finely chopped hazelnuts.

For the second baking sheet, repeat this process with the second third of the mixture, this time dusting the kisses with cocoa powder.

For the final baking sheet, crush the freeze-dried coffee into a fine powder, then mix it into the remaining third of the mixture before piping kisses onto the sheet.

Bake the meringues as per the recipe instructions (see page 15).

Make the ganache and set it aside to firm up.

Bake the cakes. Turn them out and leave them to cool completely.

Level the cakes, then stack and fill them with ganache. Place the stacked cake on a serving plate and cover it with ganache to a smooth finish. While the ganache is still sticky, carefully press the meringues into the side of cake in vertical lines, making a striped pattern, as shown.

#1

Side A: #1

TECHNIQUES

Leveling, page 18
Crumb coating, page 18
Creating a smooth finish, page 18

WHAT YOU NEED

1 rectangular (9-by-13-inch) cake (see recipes, pages 12–13)
1 quantity buttercream (see recipe, page 20)
12–15 round gummy candies in assorted colors (allowing for at least 2 of each color)
8 licorice laces

INSTRUCTIONS

Bake the cake. Turn it out and leave it to cool completely.

Make the buttercream.

TO MAKE THE #1: Level the cake. Trace the stencil onto parchment paper and cut it out. Place your stencil on the cake and cut out the shapes. Arrange your cake pieces into the 1 shape on a serving plate and stick them together with buttercream.

Crumb coat the cake with a thin layer of buttercream. Refrigerate the cake until dry to the touch, then cover the cake with buttercream to a smooth finish.

TO MAKE THE BALLOONS: Cut 1 of each color round gummy candies into 6 wedges (like you would cut a pie or a cake). Cut a tiny portion off the point of the wedges to make a flat-edged trapezoid shape. Depending on how many colors of gummy candies you are using, you will need to cut at least 2 trapezoid-shaped wedges per color. Arrange the uncut gummy candies on top of the cake as desired and add a trapezoid-shaped wedge of the same color to the bottom of each circle to complete the balloons.

Cut the licorice into 2½-inch lengths and press 1 into the buttercream at the base of each balloon.

Rolling out fondant, page 21
Coloring, page 24
Leveling, page 18
Crumb coating, page 18
Creating a smooth finish, page 18

WHAT YOU NEED

fondant: 1¾ oz white, 1¾ oz mint green & 3½ oz pink
1 rectangular (9-by-13-inch) cake (see recipes,
    pages 12–13)
1 round (10-inch) cake (see recipes, pages 12–13)
1 quantity buttercream (see recipe, page 20)
food colorings: blue & yellow
cornstarch, for rolling out fondant
1 square (1½-by-1½-inch) cutter (optional)
1 can cutter (see page 17)
1 rolling pin
4 silicone mats

#2

INSTRUCTIONS

The pinwheels can be made on the day you intend to serve the cake. Because they lie flat on the cake there is no need for them to be hard.

TO MAKE THE PINWHEELS: First form 13 small pinhead-sized balls out of white fondant. Press each ball into a flat white circle. Set the balls aside.

On a silicone mat, thinly roll out white fondant to a thickness of ⅛ inch and cut out a rectangle measuring 4 by 5 inches. Gently lift up the fondant rectangle to make sure it isn't sticking to the mat, then cut it lengthwise into ⅛-inch-wide strips. Cover the strips with another silicone mat or a damp tea towel to prevent the fondant from drying out. Repeat this process with mint green fondant.

Thinly roll out pink fondant to a thickness of ⅛ inch and cut out a rectangle measuring 5 by 8 inches. Brush the fondant with a small amount of water so that it is just damp (this will help your green and white strips stick to it). Lay the strips of white and green fondant on top of the pink, alternating the colors to create a rectangle of green and white stripes. Using a rolling pin, gently roll over the fondant, bonding the green and white strips to the pink layer (the fondant will have green and white stripes on one side and be pink on the other). Use your square cutter or a knife to cut 13 squares measuring 1½ by 1½ inches each out of this sheet of patterned fondant.

Turn half of the fondant squares upside down so that a mixture of green-and-white-striped squares and pink squares are facing upward. Using a sharp knife, cut diagonal lines from the corner of each square toward the center, leaving about ½ inch in the center uncut. Gently fold half of each corner into the center of the square and press down in the center to secure the folded corners. Repeat with all the fondant squares until you have 13 pinwheels. Use a small amount of water to stick the flat white circles onto the center of each pinwheel.

Bake the cakes. Turn them out and leave them to cool completely.

TO MAKE THE #2: Make the buttercream and color it mint green. Trace the stencil onto parchment paper and cut it out. Level the cakes to the same height and turn them over. Place the can cutter in the center of the round cake and push it all the way down through the cake to punch out the cake's middle. Discard the cake center. Place your stencil on the rectangle cake and cut out the straight pieces of the 2. Arrange the cake pieces into the 2 shape on a serving plate and stick them together using some of the buttercream. Crumb coat the cake with a thin layer of buttercream and refrigerate it until dry to the touch.

Cover the cake with buttercream to a smooth finish and place the pinwheels evenly on top of the cake.

#3

WHAT YOU NEED

1 round (8-inch) cake (see recipes, pages 12–13)
1 round (10-inch) cake (see recipes, pages 12–13)
1 quantity buttercream (see recipe, page 20)
food coloring: yellow
3 x 12.6-oz packages M&M's or similar candy-coated chocolate candies (to get 1½ cups approx. each color)

TECHNIQUES

Coloring, page 24
Creating a smooth finish, page 18

STENCIL

Side A: #3

INSTRUCTIONS

Bake the cakes. Turn them out and leave them to cool completely, dome side up. (There is no need to level the cakes.)

Make the buttercream and color it yellow.

TO MAKE THE #3: Trace the stencil onto parchment paper and cut it out. Place the stencil over the cakes and cut out the shapes. Place the cake pieces on a serving plate, arrange them into a 3 shape, and stick them together with buttercream. Use a serrated knife to round the top edges of the cakes, accentuating their natural domes.

Cover the cake with buttercream to a smooth finish.

TO DECORATE THE #3: Starting at the bottom right-hand curve of the 3, press M&M's into the buttercream in diagonal lines, alternating the colors, as shown. Continue this pattern all the way up the cake, following the curve of the cake until it is completely covered.

#4

STENCIL

Side A: #4

WHAT YOU NEED

1 rectangular (9-by-13-inch) cake (see recipes, pages 12–13)
1 quantity buttercream with a vegetable shortening base (see recipe, page 20)
food coloring: blue
9 airplane-shaped gummy candies in assorted colors
1 piping bag
1 large round tip (Wilton 6; optional)

TECHNIQUES

Coloring, page 24
Leveling, page 18
Crumb coating, page 18
Creating a smooth finish, page 18

INSTRUCTIONS

Bake the cake. Turn it out and leave it to cool completely.

Make the buttercream with a vegetable shortening base. Fit the large round tip (if using) to the piping bag, or simply cut a tiny portion off the tip of the piping bag, and fill the bag with 2 tablespoons of buttercream. Set the bag aside. Color the remaining buttercream light blue.

Level the cake, then turn it over.

TO MAKE THE #4: Trace the stencil onto parchment paper and cut it out. Place your stencil on the cake and cut out the shapes. Arrange the pieces into a 4 shape on a serving plate and stick them together with blue buttercream. Crumb coat the cake with a thin layer of blue buttercream and refrigerate the cake until dry to the touch.

TO DECORATE THE #4: Cover the cake with blue buttercream to a smooth finish, then arrange the airplane-shaped gummy candies on top of the cake, all facing in different directions.

Using the bag of uncolored buttercream, pipe 4 jet streams trailing from the back of each airplane by squeezing the frosting out in a pulsing motion.

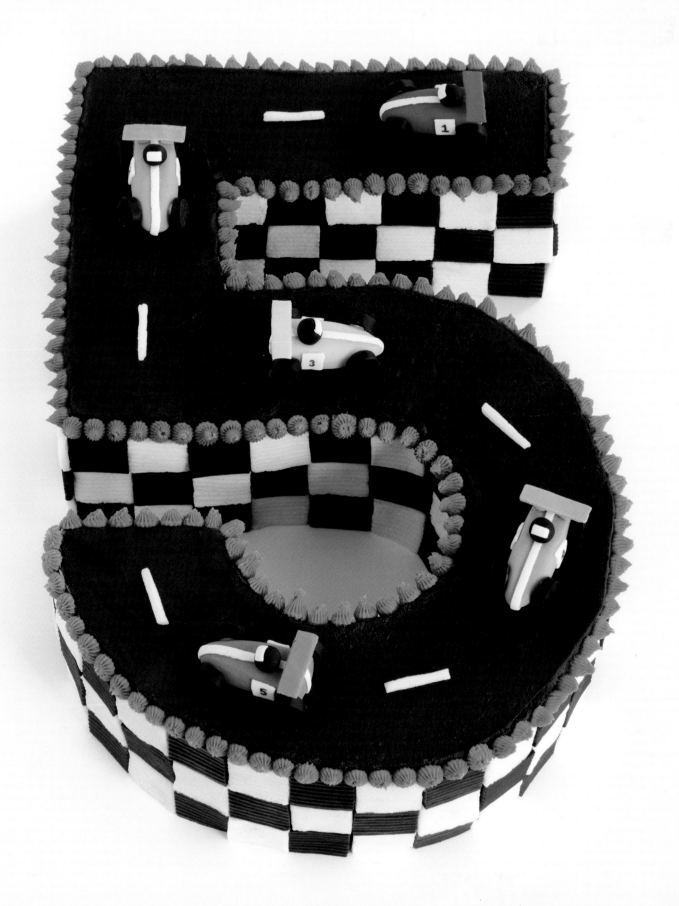

1 rectangular (9-by-13-inch) cake
  (see recipes, pages 12–13)
2 round (10-inch) cakes (see recipes, pages 12–13)
2 quantities buttercream (see recipe, page 20)
gel food colorings: black & green
fondant: 1 oz red, 1 oz orange, 1 oz yellow, 1 oz green,
  1 oz blue, 1 oz white & 1 oz black

1 x 4-inch (approx.) licorice stick
50 giant licorice allsorts
cornstarch, for rolling out fondant
1 piping bag
1 large open star tip (Wilton 199)
1 fine paintbrush
1 can cutter (see page 17)

TECHNIQUES

Rolling out fondant, page 21
Coloring, page 24
Leveling, page 18
Stacking & filling, page 18
Crumb coating, page 18
Creating a smooth finish, page 18

STENCIL

Side A: #5

INSTRUCTIONS

Bake the cakes. Turn them out and leave them to cool completely.

Make the buttercream. Set aside 1 tablespoon of uncolored buttercream, then color 3 heaped tablespoons bright green and the remaining buttercream dark gray.

TO MAKE THE RACE CARS: Thinly roll out a small amount of red fondant to a thickness of ⅛–¼ inch and cut out a ½-by-1¼-inch rectangular spoiler. From the remaining red fondant, form 2 balls the size of pinheads and shape the rest into a 2-inch-long car shape. Use a small amount of water to stick the 2 pinhead balls to the back of the car, then stick the spoiler piece on top of the balls. Repeat this process with the orange, yellow, green, and blue fondant to make all 5 cars. For the helmets, roll the black fondant into 5 pea-sized balls. Thinly roll out the white fondant to a thickness of ⅛ inch and cut out 5 strips ⅛ inch wide. Use a small amount of water to stick a stripe down the middle of each race car. Cut a leftover strip into tiny rectangles and use a dot of water to stick one to the front of each black pea-sized helmet. Use a small amount of water to stick the small helmets in front of each spoiler, on top of the white stripe. Finally, from the leftover white fondant cut out 10 small squares. Use a small amount of water to stick a square to both sides of each car. Number the sides of the cars from 1 to 5 using the paintbrush and black food coloring. For the wheels, cut the licorice sticks into 20 thin slices no thicker than ¼ inch. Use a small amount of uncolored buttercream to stick 4 wheels to each car, then set the cars aside.

TO MAKE THE #5: Level the cakes to the same height and turn them over. Place the can cutter in the center of one of the round cakes and push all the way down through the cake to punch out the middle. Discard the cake center and repeat this process with the other round cake. Trace the stencil onto parchment paper and cut it out. Place your stencil on the rectangle cake and cut out 2 sets of the straight pieces of the 5. Place your stencil on one of the round cakes and cut the bottom section out of the 5 where the circle meets the straight edges. Repeat this process with the other round cake. Arrange 1 circular piece and 1 set of straight pieces on a serving plate and stick them together using some of the dark gray buttercream. Cover this first layer with dark gray buttercream, then stack the second layer on top, sticking the top circular piece and straight pieces together at the same time. Crumb coat the stacked cake with a thin layer of dark gray buttercream, then refrigerate it until dry to the touch.

TO MAKE THE CHECKERBOARD PATTERN: Separate the layers of the giant licorice allsorts. Discard the colored layers and retain only the white layers and the black licorice layers, gently washing and drying them if necessary. Cover the cake with dark gray buttercream to a smooth finish. Press the white and black licorice allsorts squares into the buttercream around the sides of the cake in a checkerboard pattern.

TO MAKE THE ROAD: Fit the large open star tip to a piping bag and fill the bag with the green buttercream you set aside earlier. Pipe green dots all around the upper edge of the cake, as shown.

Evenly space the cars on top of the cake. Cut some of the leftover white licorice allsorts layers into strips and place them between the cars as road markings.

Notes

When coloring buttercream dark gray, use black gel coloring to achieve a darker result.

You can use small toy cars if you do not want to make the fondant cars.

#6

1 quantity meringue kisses (see recipe, page 15)

gel food colorings: blue, green, orange, purple, red & yellow

1 rectangular (9-by-13-inch) cake (see recipes, pages 12–13)

1 round (8-inch) cake (see recipes, pages 12–13)

1 quantity buttercream (see recipe, page 20)

1¼ cups multicolor sprinkles

1 piping bag

1 extra-large round tip (Wilton 1A)

1 paintbrush

1 can cutter (see page 17)

3 baking sheets

STENCIL

Side A: #6

TECHNIQUES

Leveling, page 18

Crumb coating, page 18

Creating a smooth finish, page 18

INSTRUCTIONS

Make the meringue kisses at least a day in advance of serving the cake.

TO MAKE THE STRIPY MERINGUE KISSES: Make the meringue mixture.

Fit the extra-large round tip to the piping bag and turn the bag inside out. Use the paintbrush to paint evenly spaced ½-inch-wide gel stripes in vertical lines on the inside-out bag. Start the stripes inside the tip, then paint all the way up the piping bag, stopping 2 inches from the top. Paint the colors in the same order as a rainbow—red, orange, yellow, green, blue, and purple. Turn the bag back the right way around, being careful not to smudge the gel stripes. Completely fill the piping bag with the meringue mixture and pipe small kisses with a 1¼-inch base onto the baking sheet, keeping them as uniform in size and shape as possible. To make a kiss shape, squeeze until the circle is the size of the base you want, then release the pressure and pull up to create a peak on the kiss. As you squeeze out the meringue mixture it will pull the color through the piping tip and paint rainbow stripes on each kiss.

Fill the baking sheets with colorful kisses. Bake the meringues as per the recipe instructions (see page 15).

Bake the cakes. Turn them out and leave them to cool completely.

Make the buttercream.

Level the cakes to the same height and turn them over.

TO MAKE THE #6: Place the can cutter in the center of the round cake and push it all the way down through the cake to punch out the middle. Discard the cake center. Trace the stencil onto parchment paper and cut it out. Place your stencil on the cake and cut the edge off around the circular cake.

Place the stencil on the rectangle cake and cut out the stem for the 6. Arrange the cake pieces into a 6 shape on a serving plate and stick them together using some of the buttercream. Crumb coat the cake with a thin layer of buttercream, then refrigerate it until dry to the touch.

Add as many sprinkles as you desire to the remaining buttercream, mixing them in until just combined. Cover the cake in buttercream to a smooth finish.

Arrange the meringues on top of the cake, as shown.

Note

To ensure the meringue kisses are all the same size, draw circles the size of a quarter onto parchment paper and use these as a guide when you pipe each kiss.

1 rectangular (9-by-13-inches) cake
(see recipes, pages 12–13)
2 quantities buttercream (see recipe, page 20)
food coloring: red
1 piping bag
1 extra-large star tip (Wilton 1M)

STENCIL

Side A: #7

TECHNIQUES

Leveling, page 18
Crumb coating, page 18
Piping techniques (rosettes), page 28

INSTRUCTIONS

Bake the cake. Turn it out and leave it to cool completely.

Make the buttercream. Add just a few drops of red food coloring to it, then mix it to create a very pale pink color.

TO MAKE THE #7: Trace the stencil onto parchment paper and cut it out. Level the cake, then turn it over. Place your stencil on the cake and cut out the 7 shape. Place the cake pieces on a serving plate and stick them together with buttercream. Crumb coat the cake with a thin layer of pale pink buttercream, then refrigerate the cake until dry to the touch.

TO DECORATE THE #7: Fit the extra-large star tip to the piping bag and half fill the bag with the pale pink buttercream. Starting at the bottom of the cake, pipe 2 rosettes on the top surface, 1 down each side of the cake and 2 on the front edge.

Make sure the rosettes are big enough that there are no gaps in between and that the cake is covered to the bottom edge.

Squeeze the leftover buttercream in the piping bag back into the bowl. Mix a couple more drops of red food coloring into the bowl of buttercream to make a slightly brighter shade of pink, as shown, and refill the piping bag. Pipe the next line of rosettes, on the top surface and down the sides, above the first row.

Repeat this process all the way up the cake, slowly adding and mixing in more food coloring each time, creating an ombré effect from pale pink to bright pink.

#8

INSTRUCTIONS

Make the ganache and set it aside to firm up.

Bake the cakes. Turn them out and leave them to cool completely.

TO MAKE THE #8: Level the cakes to 1½ inches high each. Stack and fill 2 cakes with ganache, then repeat this process with the other 2 cakes so that you end up with 2 stacked cakes. Place the can cutter in the center of each cake stack and push all the way down through the cake to punch out the middle. Discard the cake centers.

Cut a straight-edged slice off each cake stack, approximately ½ inch in from the edge. Place the 2 cake stacks on a serving plate and stick the flat edges together with ganache to create an 8 shape.

TO DECORATE THE #8: Carefully cut or break Kit Kat bars into single wafers. Cover the cake with ganache to a smooth finish, then press Kit Kat wafers into the ganache all the way around the outside of the cake. (The Kit Kats will stand up higher than the cake.) Gently tie string or ribbon around the wafers to hold them in place until the ganache dries. Press wafers into the insides of the cut-out circles, as shown.

Arrange M&M's on the top of the cake, as shown, or simply pour them in randomly.

Remove the ribbon or string once the ganache has dried and the wafers are firmly attached.

Notes
A single-level cake can be made with just 2 x 8-inch cakes.

Cut the KitKat bars 3 inches long to make a shorter outer edge.

STENCIL

Side A: #8 (optional)

WHAT YOU NEED

2 quantities dark chocolate ganache (see recipe, page 21)
4 round (8-inch) cakes (see recipes, pages 12–13)
22 x 1½-oz packages Kit Kat bars (or 88 wafers)
4 x 12.6-oz packages M&M's or similar candy-coated chocolate candies
1 can cutter (see page 17)
1 piece ribbon or string

TECHNIQUES

Leveling, page 18
Creating a smooth finish, page 18
Stacking & filling, page 18

#9

WHAT YOU NEED

1 rectangular (9-by-13-inch) cake (see recipes, pages 12–13)

1 round (8-inch) cake (see recipes, pages 12–13)

1 quantity buttercream (see recipe, page 20)

food coloring: blue & yellow

fondant: 5 oz white

cornstarch, for rolling out fondant

1 daisy-shaped cutter (see page 17)

1 can cutter (see page 17)

1 piping bag

1 large round tip (Wilton 6)

TECHNIQUES

Leveling, page 18

Crumb coating, page 18

Creating a smooth finish, page 18

Rolling out fondant, page 21

STENCIL

Side A: #9

INSTRUCTIONS

Bake the cakes. Turn them out and leave them to cool completely.

Make the buttercream. Place 2 heaped tablespoons in a separate bowl, color it yellow, and set it aside. Color the remaining buttercream blue.

Level the cakes to the same height and turn them upside down.

TO MAKE THE #9: Place the can cutter in the center of the round cake and push it all the way down through the cake to punch out the middle. Discard the cake center. Trace the stencil onto parchment paper and cut it out. Place the stencil on the cake and, using it as a guide, cut off the edge around the circular cake.

Place the stencil on the rectangle cake and cut out the stem of the 9. Arrange the cake pieces into a 9 shape on a serving plate and stick them together using some of the blue buttercream.

Crumb coat the cake with a thin layer of blue buttercream, then refrigerate it until dry to the touch.

Cover the cake with blue buttercream to a smooth finish.

TO MAKE THE DAISIES: Thinly roll out white fondant to a thickness of 1/8 inch. Dip the daisy-shaped cutter in cornstarch, then press it into the fondant to cut out a daisy shape. Repeat this process until you have 21 fondant daisies. Arrange the daisies on top of the cake, spacing them evenly.

Fit the large round tip to the piping bag and fill it with the yellow buttercream you set aside earlier. Pipe a small yellow center in the middle of each flower.

#10

Bake the cakes. Turn them out and leave them to cool completely.

Make the buttercream, mix in cocoa powder, then color the buttercream black.

Make the royal icing and set it aside, covering the bowl with plastic wrap to prevent the icing from drying out.

Level the cakes to the same height and turn them over.

TO MAKE THE #10: Place the can cutter in the center of the round cake and push it all the way down through the cake to punch out the middle. Discard the cake center. Cut the cake in half.

Trace the stencils onto parchment paper and cut them out. Using the stencils as your guide, cut the straight sections of the 1 and the 0 from the rectangle cake.

Put all the cake pieces, including the round halves, on a serving plate and arrange them into a 10. Stick the pieces together with buttercream.

Crumb coat the cakes with a thin layer of buttercream and refrigerate them until dry to the touch.

Cover the cakes with buttercream to a smooth finish.

TO DECORATE THE #10: Fit the small round tip to the piping bag and fill the bag with white royal icing. Pipe a thin, continuous wiggly line all over the top of the cake in a random fashion. Do not let the lines touch. Practice on some parchment paper first, if you wish. Be patient and give your hands a break when they need it—this takes a while but is well worth the effort!

WHAT YOU NEED

1 rectangular (9-by-13-inch) cake (see recipes, pages 12–13)

1 round (8-inch) cake (see recipes, pages 12–13)

2 quantities buttercream (see recipe, page 20)

5 tbsp cocoa powder

gel food coloring: black

1 quantity royal icing (see recipe, page 20)

1 can cutter (see page 17)

1 piping bag

1 small round tip (Wilton 3)

TECHNIQUES

Coloring, page 24

Leveling, page 18

Crumb coating, page 18

Creating a smooth finish, page 18

STENCILS

Side A: #1 & #0

INDEX

Almost all the cakes and cupcakes in this book can be made using either the vanilla or chocolate cake recipes on pages 12 and 13. We recommend that all princess and hemisphere cakes in this book be made using the chocolate cake recipe.

80 Cakes LATER & STILL Smiling!

Jaz
DAUGHTER-IN-LAW

Wendy
MOTHER-IN-LAW

ACKNOWLEDGMENTS

What a treat it has been to work with Murray Thom and the wonderful team at Thom Productions. You are all such encouragers, and I am very grateful for your belief in me. I'd especially like to thank Tim Harper for inviting me to the project and for giving me the confidence to follow my instincts.

Thank you to Dean Brettschneider for your delicious recipes. It was an honor to work with you. Thank you also to Michelle Pattison for your valuable baking advice and notes.

To the publishing teams at Weldon Owen and PQ Blackwell, thank you for your enthusiastic support and for your commitment to producing a book we can all be incredibly proud of.

To my Nixon family—Grant, Wendy, Grace—I can't possibly list everything you have done to help bring this book to life or thank you enough for your constant encouragement. You've kept me fed, cleaned up the mess, put up with late nights and early mornings, and dashed to the shops "just one more time"—all without complaint. You're the best.

To my family—Grant, Kim, Hannah, and Nana Barbara Lynch, thank you for encouraging me to express my creativity through cake decorating and for tolerating years of being kept awake until late at night while I practiced my craft. I wouldn't have made it this far without you.

To my UP Real Estate "family," especially Grant, Barry, Brad, Manu, and Simon, thank you for putting up with me thinking about sugary things and for covering for me so I could meet my deadlines!

To Mum and Mary Wells, thanks for being our "eagle eyes" and reading the book before it went for editing. To Nana Margaret, thanks for all the Monday-night dinners and for attending to the important little jobs like sorting candies into colors and washing licorice squares.

To Lottie Hedley, what more can I say other than that your photographs make my cakes shine, and to Hayley Thom, your videos brought the entire process to life.

To Henry Harper, whose second birthday was the initial inspiration for this book and whose little hand appears on the back cover, and his mom, Tali, thank you.

To Churchill Park School, particularly Carolyn Neary and the children from Room 10, thank you for your enthusiasm for our cakes and for giving them such delightful names. To the Poole family and their friends, thanks for allowing us to photograph and enjoy Coco's fifth birthday party. To Chrissy Conyngham, thank you for opening up your gorgeous home for our final photography session.

Finally, I thank God for my wonderful husband and chief cake taste-tester, Josh. I will always treasure your unconditional love and support. Thank you for encouraging me to take on this exciting challenge.

I am very grateful to you all.

Blessings,
Jaz

weldon**owen**

Published in North America by Weldon Owen
1045 Sansome Street, San Francisco, CA 94111
www.weldonowen.com
Weldon Owen is a division of Bonnier Publishing USA

This edition printed in 2017

Produced for Weldon Owen by PQ Blackwell, New Zealand

Copyright © 2017 PQ Blackwell Limited pqblackwell.com
Thom Productions Limited thomproductions.com

Portions of this book were originally published as
The Great New Zealand Birthday Cake Book
Copyright © 2016 PQ Blackwell Limited pqblackwell.com
Thom Productions Limited thomproductions.com

ISBN: 978-1-68188-239-0

Printed in China by 1010 Printing Group Limited
10 9 8 7 6 5 4 3 2 1

CAKE DESIGNER: Jazmine Nixon
RECIPES: Dean Brettschneider
EDITOR: Wendy Nixon
BAKING CONSULTANT: Michelle Pattison

EXECUTIVE PRODUCER: Murray Thom
CREATIVE DIRECTOR: Tim Harper

PHOTOGRAPHY: Lottie Hedley
VIDEOGRAPHER: Hayley Thom
RETOUCHER: Daryl Simonson

PUBLISHER: Geoff Blackwell
EDITOR-IN-CHIEF: Ruth Hobday
DESIGN: Tim Harper
ADDITIONAL DESIGN: Jenny Moore
EDITORIAL: Rachel Clare
ADDITIONAL EDITORIAL: Kimberley Davis & Susan Brookes

Find and follow Jazmine on Instagram: @jazminenixoncakes

Find and follow Dean at: globalbaker.com

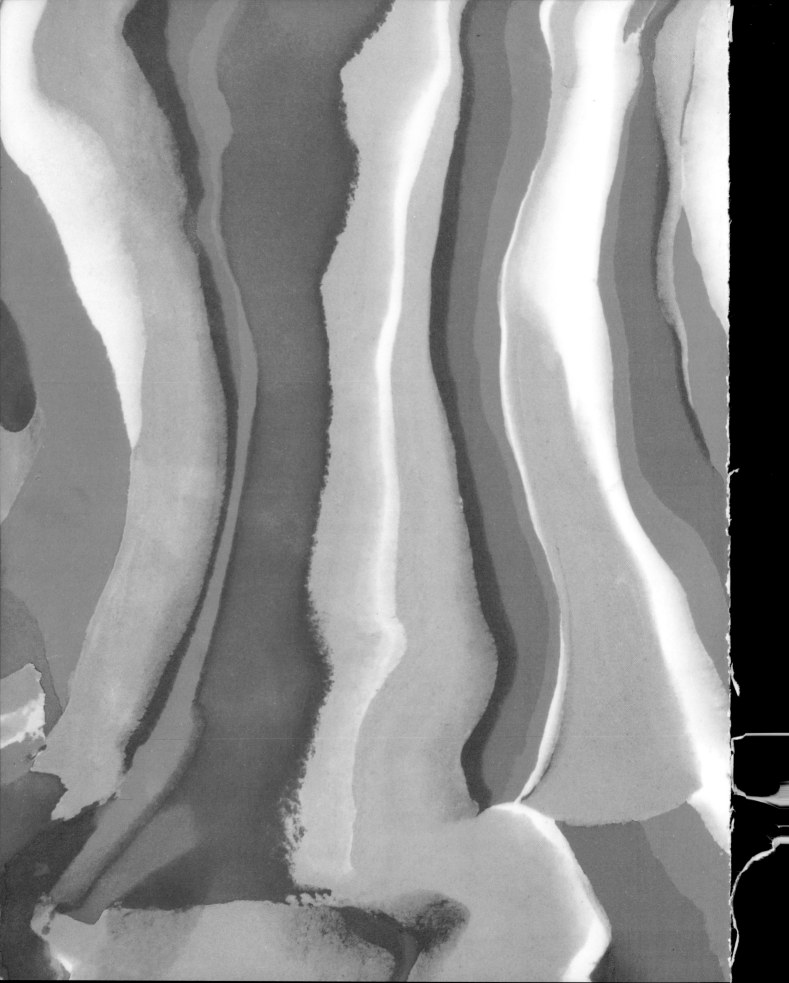